KEEPING THE BEAT

Barry Whitwam, Keeping the beat
Copyright © Barry Whitwam & Nunatak A/S, 2025
Publisher: Nunatak A/S
Cover Artwork: Kenneth Dokkeberg, Dokkeberg Design
Editor: Stig Ulrichsen
1st Edition, 1st Printing
ISBN: 978-87-92840-33-2

A lot of effort has been made to trace copyright holders and obtain their permission for the use of copyrighted photos and material. The publisher apologises for any errors or omissions and would be grateful to be notified of any corrections that should be incorporated in future reprints or editions of this book.

BARRY WHITWAM

KEEPING THE BEAT

MY LIFE WITH HERMAN'S HERMITS

I would like to express my heartfelt gratitude to my wonderful wife, Pat, and my family for their unwavering support and patience during all those years I spent on the road.

FOREWORD

The first verse from the lyrics of East West, a song written by Graham Gouldman for Herman's Hermits in 1966, sums up pretty well drummer Barry Whitwam's life on the road with the band:

"East, West, over the ocean, perpetual motion, travelling around, no rest, singing and playing, night out and day in, doing the rounds, what a great life it must seem…"

Barry has been the drummer with Herman's Hermits ever since April 1964. Just a few months later the group's debut single for Columbia (EMI), I'm Into Something Good, shot to No. 1 in the UK charts. The group became one of the most successful acts on the 60s music scene, notching up more than 20 hit singles on both sides of the Atlantic. Many of their albums for MGM also qualified for Gold Record awards in the US. Total sales are estimated to more than 80 million records worldwide — in 1965 Herman's Hermits sold more records than anybody else, including The Beatles! As a live act they filled stadiums and played to sell-out audiences at prestigious theatres and club venues everywhere. Topping the bill, Herman's Hermits were touring endlessly, especially in

America, often bringing along other British bands such as The Animals, Wayne Fontana & The Mindbenders and The Hollies as support acts. 1967 even saw the unlikely pairing of Herman's Hermits with The Who as warm-up band on an infamous American tour, which got both groups banned from the Holiday Inn hotel chain everywhere.

The music of Herman's Hermits had universal appeal. Hermania quickly spread across the globe — from the UK to USA and Canada, Australia and New Zealand, Europe, The Middle East, Asia, Central America, South America and Africa. The boys from Manchester conquered the world — including old Viking territory just across the North Sea — my home country of Norway and the rest of Scandinavia.

When No Milk Today reached No. 1 in Norway, the Hermits paid a visit to Oslo for TV and concert appearances in early 1967. I was only 12 then, and I got my first record player — a portable Philips Bambino plus a couple of Herman's Hermits 45s to go with it. I played those singles over and over again — and as soon as I had saved up weekly allowances to buy a few Herman's Hermits LPs including the landmark album Blaze, there was no looking back. I had become a superfan and collector of everything to do with Herman's Hermits. If someone had told me back then that my interest in pop music and record collecting would later lead to lifelong friendships with members of my favourite band, I would surely have laughed and thought they were joking. Something like that just seemed too unlikely to ever happen. Yet it did come true a few years later, and the sequence of events that made it happen is given by Barry in a chapter of this book.

By then, in the mid-1970s, the hits had sadly stopped coming for Herman's Hermits, still I remained a loyal fan and collector, buying everything I could find from all corners of the world. Of the original members Peter Noone had left to pursue a solo career in 1971, Keith Hopwood followed suit a year later to build up Pluto Recording Studios in Manchester and concentrate on writing and producing jingles and music for television. Karl Green left in 1980 to set up a tiling business and later also started a PA hire company in London. Derek Leckenby played in Herman's Hermits until 1994, when he sadly died of Non-Hodgkin lymphoma. Since then, original drummer Barry Whitwam has soldiered on with Herman's Hermits decade after decade. Despite inevitable line-up changes over the years, he has managed to keep the band going as a tight, hard-working unit of professional musicians to this day.

Barry is not only a brilliant drummer, he is also a great showman and entertainer. In the 70s he started taking a more prominent role in the band's stage shows with a magic act, some crude jokes and some nonsense poetry to go with it. There was also a ten-minute drum solo during Truck Stop Momma which took him from the drum kit and through the audience, playing on everything from tables to wine glasses without missing a beat. The audiences loved it. In more recent years, Barry's drum solo during the Sandy Nelson instrumental Let There Be Drums is still a favourite in the set.

For 60 years Barry has travelled non-stop, thousands and thousands of miles throughout the world, keeping the beat behind the drums and giving pleasure and enjoyment to capacity audiences wherever the band has appeared. He can look back on a remarkable career with one of the most successful pop groups of the 60s, who sold millions of records, starred in three major movies for MGM and appeared on countless popular TV shows.

Barry's autobiography gives a very honest and humorous account of life on the road with Herman's Hermits. One of the things that has kept him going for so long is obviously a wonderful sense of humour. A lot of the behind-the-scenes stories in this book are really hilarious and guaranteed to make you laugh. But he also shares memories tinged with sadness and loss.

Even though a trademark for Herman's Hermits has always been cheerful, melodic pop songs, a sunshine pop group won't necessarily be blessed with sunny days all the time. In a touring band there will always be challenges to face and problems of all kinds to resolve. But nothing as severe and completely out of one's hands as the covid-19 pandemic, which hit the world in 2020 and sadly prevented the band from touring for more than a year. Obviously not an easy situation to deal with for a hard-working touring band. But the itch to play and entertain people was never lost, and the summer of 2021 saw Herman's Hermits back in business again.

In 2024 Herman's Hermits marked their 60th. Anniversary with a World Tour that took them from England to Spain,

Norway, Australia, Denmark, Germany and a number of other countries. The interest in the music of Herman's Hermits remains strong around the world and will no doubt keep the band busy touring for many years to come.

Thank you so much, Barry — keep on rockin', mate!

Olaf Owre
January 2025

1

Beginnings

My mother was convinced I was going to be a girl, so much so that she had already decided upon a name – Yvonne. So, when I arrived as a healthy boy, it disrupted her plans enough to send her into a quandary.

I was born in Prestbury, Cheshire. Manchester was bombed so heavily during the Second World War that many temporary maternity units had been created, and placed far from the danger of Nazi bombs. The hospital registrar had paid several visits to my mother in the hope that she had decided upon a name, but to no avail. When, on the fifth day the registrar pressed her for a name, my mother was listening to a tune on the radio. As the music finished, the presenter announced that it was the Jan Barry Orchestra, and my name was decided in that instant: Jan Barry Whitwam – born 21st July, 1946.

"Let's just call him Barry, shall we," the registrar suggested, but my mother was insistent, and I was named after an orchestra.

Naturally, I have always concurred with the registrar's wisdom, and the Jan has remained mostly superfluous. When you're waiting for a prescription in a doctor's surgery, the receptionist shouts out 'Jan Whitwam', and a strapping six-footer stands up, you're guaranteed a selection of choice looks.

When I was six-years-old, I made the mistake of confiding in my best school friend, and, after much coaxing told him what the 'J' stood for. In spite of him promising on his mother's life that he would keep my secret, within five minutes everybody in the school knew my real name, and I was referred to as 'Jam Butty Whitwam' thereafter. Children can be so cruel. Like the narrator in A Boy Named Sue, I ended up in many fights because of that name. What a way to step out into the world…

My interest in playing the drums started in a way that most schoolboys will recognise. When I was about thirteen-years-old, five boys in my neighbourhood started a group. Equipped with three guitars, a bass guitar, and some cardboard boxes to hit, they approached me and said that I could join…if I could get a set of drums. Of course, this seemed like a fantastic plan to me, so I went to work on softening my mother to the idea. It took me a week of promising to repay the money before she was on my side, that just left the biggest hurdle…dad.

At around the same time that my interest in playing drums was sparked, tragedy hit our family. In 1959, my elder brother, Trevor, was killed when he accidentally electrocuted himself in the bath. He had perched a Dansette record player on the side of the tub so that he could listen to his favourite music while bathing. Perhaps he too had visions of being a famous musician, but sadly we'll never know what he might have achieved.

My mother was the unfortunate person to find him, and, naturally, we were all distraught. But this tragic event partly informed my dad's decision to allow me a drum kit, as he acknowledged that I was now an only child, and in spite of money always being tight, my parents decided that they must do everything in their power to support my pursuits. 1959 was a very formative year.

When I was growing up, Oxford Road in Manchester was a hive of happening music shops; there were seven or eight great shops within half a mile of each other, and like every other boy of my age, I spent my Saturday mornings looking through the windows of these shops, hypnotically gawping at the shiny instruments. Strangely enough, it was only when my friends asked me to join the band that I started to look at the drums.

My parents were friendly with the owners of one of the shops, the now legendary Stock & Chapman. My mother arranged with Ma Chapman that we could afford to spend about £40 (on hire purchase) on a set of drums, which I worked out I could repay within about 2 years, courtesy of my paper round and some car-washing jobs. Excitedly I started to look at the sparkling drum kits in the shop window, wondering which one I would get. Ma Chapman returned from the basement with an assistant and presented me with what can only be described as a mongrel drum kit; there was a President bass drum, an Olympic tom-tom, an Ajax snare – my first kit was made by five different manufacturers!

On the bright side, all of the drums were a similar shade of off-white, so they looked as if they belonged together from a distance. In addition to the shells there was a cymbal with a huge crack in it, and a ride cymbal full of rivets. The riveted cymbal was a remnant of the jazz era, but a lot of rock 'n' roll drummers still used them, so I felt in good company.

So, that was my first drum set, and with a lot of car polish and elbow grease, I had the kit shining like a shilling.

I couldn't wait to get stuck in. After excitedly setting up our equipment in the front room at one of the lad's houses, we began playing. It was at this exact moment in time that I realised I had a problem: I couldn't play the drums. I have no idea why, but for some reason I expected everything to sound amazing the second we started, but it was a terrible racket. It wasn't until five months later that I realised why I found it so difficult. After a gig, one of the boys said to me:

"I thought you were right-handed, Barry?" to which I replied that I was.

"So, why do you set your kit up left-handed?"

And there it was – for the first five months of my drumming career I'd been playing with the kit set up entirely wrong. Set up correctly, I was delighted to find that I could actually play the drums, and it was probably just in time, as the other lads were quickly running out of patience with me.

To celebrate this enlightenment, I decided to take some drum lessons with a chap called Ken Leyland, who had a teaching room in the basement of Stock & Chapman's. I did this for eighteen months, and it was, without question, one of the best decisions I ever made. Ken focused on the rudiments, teaching me to play only on a rubber pad (this is still how I practise and warm-up to this very day), and in a year and a half I never once got to play the kit he had set up in his room, in anger or otherwise. Instead, he would give me an exercise from the Buddy Rich snare drum rudiments book, and I would return the week after and attempt to play it to him. Progress may have been slow, but as a band we were starting to get bookings at youth clubs and social clubs in and around Manchester.

The story of teenage hopefuls has never changed, and it was only thanks to my father and one of the other fathers that we managed to transport us and our equipment to shows. Without their support, we would never have left the house. You would invariably end up on a backseat wedged between a drum kit and a bass amp with a microphone stand in your face, but those were very happy days.

So, we had equipment, transport and some shows. At this juncture it's worth pointing out the other vital ingredients necessary to make it in show business, without which, the struggle becomes almost impossible. Firstly, a never-ending supply of enthusiasm is essential. When you first start out, particularly, the knocks come thick and fast – there are just as many people telling you that you'll never make it as there are encouraging you, so a blind, wilful obstinance is your greatest weapon. And the greatest accompaniment to enthusiasm is an unbreakable sense of humour – there are some situations when this will be your only saviour. And I suppose a little talent doesn't go amiss…

These formative experiences, like being crushed into vehicles, held us in very good stead for the years on the road that would follow, but more about that later.

I am now fourteen-years-old, and two years down the long road to fame and fortune. We were sounding good. Like so many bands at the time, we were a four-piece (two guitars, bass and drums) and had, until now, only ever played instrumental tunes by the likes of The Ventures, The Shadows and Duane Eddy. It was at this point that we decided we needed a singer, and, after some enquiries we were introduced to Brian (we never did know his last name), and by virtue of his less than towering 4' 10" build, he quickly became known as 'Little Bry'. The band was called The Demons at that time, and collectively agreeing that 'Brian & The Demons' didn't quite have that special ring to it, so we changed Brian's name for him and we became 'Danny & The Demons'. Now, there was a name to conquer the world…

By the late fifties, jazz was beginning to fizzle out only to be replaced by a more vibrant club scene in which the pop groups were taking over. This was good news for guys like us. I have nothing against jazz, but that was not a world in which we could compete. But in this new regime, it meant that we were getting shows further afield, and not just around Manchester. And we were on the up…we could now afford to pay a local shopkeeper to run us to and from gigs in his van. This was how real bands toured.

I recall, with warm amusement, a show we played at the Damon Hotel in Doncaster. The north of England is divided, somewhat dramatically, by the Pennine Hills, which reach a chilly and often windy 1800 feet. With Manchester to the west and Doncaster to the east, this was by far the furthest we'd travelled to a show as yet, a round trip of some 160 miles. With our arrival a little later than anticipated we threw our equipment onto the stage in an attempt to be ready for our eight o'clock performance. The hotel manager said that the house P.A. would probably be better than ours, which was absolutely correct as our P.A. was the bass player's amp. However, the peculiarity of the house P.A. was that it had been set up for the benefit of jazz bands, which meant there was a single microphone suspended above the stage hanging from the ceiling at a height of about six feet or so.

The Demons went on stage and opened with an instrumental tune, which received warm enough applause. Then we gave Little Bry a nice big introduction:

"Ladies and gentlemen, please give a huge welcome to Danny!"

The audience gave him enthusiastic applause as we broke into the opening bars of Elvis Presley's Jailhouse Rock.

What happened next will remain one of the funniest moments of my life. Little Bry ran onto the stage looking for the microphone stand, but of course there wasn't one. As he continued to dash around the stage in panic, we motioned that the microphone was above him.

"Look up you idiot, the mic is hanging from the ceiling," I shouted.

Thanks to his severe lack of height though, he was some distance short of being able to reach it. But Little Bry was persistent, if nothing else, and proceeded to jump up and down as he sung in his efforts to be amplified, but this gallant yet somewhat pitiful technique resulted in the audience only hearing every fourth word of the song. I started to laugh, the rest of the band started to laugh, and more crucially the audience started to laugh. Within seconds the place was on its knees – the more they laughed, the more we did. With the room in a state of mirth, the song had to stop.

The only people not laughing were Little Bry and the red-faced manager.

"I thought I'd hired a rock 'n' roll band, not a comedy band," he shouted across the stage at us.

Fearful that we would be paid off right there and then, I dashed to the dressing room and came back with an empty beer crate for Bry to stand on.

"Fuck off," he uttered on my return, but when I explained the gig would be over if he didn't, he reluctantly complied and stepped onto the crate. There were complaints and protests from him between songs, but we got through the show with our lead singer standing on a pale ale crate.

The drive home was almost as eventful. Halfway across the Pennines, it was becoming increasingly more likely that a toilet stop would be needed, and because of heavy snow and a furious wind, it was decided that one coordinated stop should be made. As the driver and I simultaneously opened the front doors, a 40mph wind ripped through the cabin and took with it everything that was on the dashboard, including the road tax disc. I blithely decided to give chase, but the disc sailed over the side of the Pennines into the blustery dark, never to be seen again. I laughed uncontrollably, as I tend to when things go wrong, but the driver was far from happy, and shortly after informed us that he could no longer do the job. He was replaced by a sixty-year-old coffin-maker, and while we didn't mind that he used his van to carry coffins by day and musicians by night, we did object to whatever the vile concoction was that he smoked in his pipe. We would arrive at venues stinking of smoky shit, and gleaning looks of disgust from the public. We knew he wouldn't last long…

Little Bry's tenure, too, was coming to a close. An avid Manchester United supporter, he had already told us that he wouldn't rehearse on Saturday afternoons if his chosen team were playing at home, and to make matters worse, he'd also started to bring his girlfriend to gigs. It was time for a band meeting (a band meeting nearly always meant that somebody was about to get the push).

And so we told Brian that he would have to rehearse the following Saturday, knowing that he would tell us to get stuffed. He did just that.

Within days we'd found a replacement for Brian. I struggle to recall his real name, but courtesy of his slightly dark skin he was soon answering to the name 'Sabu'. These were very different times. Then, of course, it was obligatory to find him a stage name, and the best we could come up with was 'The Unknown', so we became The Demons with the Unknown.

It's remarkable how, no matter how brilliant an idea seemed at the time, in retrospect you realise it was in fact stupid.

The Unknown also struggled to fit our dynamic because he too was seemingly never without his girlfriend. As much as we all like girls, it makes maintaining the unity of a band very difficult when the lads are holding hands and petting, and not indulging in the general banter and togetherness of the journey. Perhaps my interests were too firmly entrenched in the fun aspect back then.

I remember once pulling up outside my girlfriend's house in my Morris van a few years later to tell her that I couldn't see her because I had something else to do. I was in fact going boating, but I didn't want her to know that.

But of course she saw the boat strapped to the roof of my van.

"What's that boat doing on the roof?" she quizzed.

"What boat?" I shouted, and drove off laughing to myself.

As it turned out, I drove about a mile before the clutch went on the van, and never got to go boating after all. It was probably a blessing as I had made the boat myself from what can only be described as somewhat 'sketchy' plans.

The boat did eventually get her maiden voyage, some three months later, when a friend and I went to Wales on a fishing trip. As I said, I had made this boat myself, and it's worth pointing out that she was seven feet long, and both the bow and stern were perfectly square – it resembled a small child's drawing of a boat.

My friend had convinced me that to be good fishermen we needed live bait, so we went on the hunt for lugworms. To catch a lugworm, one must find a worm cast in the wet sand by the water's edge, and then dig as fast as is humanly possible. After two hours of digging, we'd probably moved over a ton of sand, but not seen a single lugworm. So we ended up going with my original suggestion of going to the bait shop and buying some dried worms.

We were all set; we had all of our fishing gear, some bait, sandwiches and a dry cloth in case it rained. We dragged the boat into the water and excitedly jumped in, and prepared to be powered by our own oars. The first small wave that hit the square front filled the boat with water in five seconds flat. The day was a disaster, and it was another four years before I braved the water again, this time on Lake Windermere, in my new seventeen-foot sailing boat, a boat that had been built by people who knew what they were doing.

Sabo lasted about six months before we had another band meeting, and so, not for the first time, or the last, we became a band without a singer. In fact, of the myriad singers we had, only one of them – Geoff Mullins – left the band voluntarily. Geoff had been our manager at one stage, and turned up at clubs to get us gigs in his white suit and black 1934 Rolls Royce. He looked quite the part. But his last evening with us as a singer came at a hotel in Llandudno, Wales.

When we arrived, we were told by the management that we had to play three forty-five minute spots, which was a little tricky for us, as we barely had enough material to fill two such spots. Repeats were inevitable.

In the third set, Geoff turned to me for song ideas, at which I suggest I'm a Hog For You Baby.

"We've played that twice already," Geoff shouted back.

"It'll be fine," I reply, "it's a great rocker!"

"If you play that song again, I'm leaving the band," Geoff said.

I counted the song in, and Geoff marched off stage and out of the band. We began the gig as a four-piece band, and finished the night as a three-piece band.

Still, we got paid and the management enjoyed us so much we got a rebooking out of it. We couldn't convince Geoff to stay with us, which was a shame because he owned the P.A. system, and he point blank refused to sell it to us. To add to the evening's misery, when we got home we realised that we'd left our stage boots at the venue, so Lek and I had to drive back to North Wales the next day to retrieve them.

Shortly after, another friend of ours, named Dave Chalmers – who, incidentally was going to be the drummer of The Demons if he'd bought a drum kit before I did – said he would like to be the driver/roadie for the band. Who needs a singer when you've got a roadie?

Within a few days he turned up with a battleship grey Austin J2 van that he'd bought from a building contractor for the princely sum of £40. The next few days were spent rearranging the seats and cleaning all of the muck out. We had another meeting – this time to change the name of the band to The Wailers – and Dave painted the new name down each side of the group van.

By this time in 1963, The Wailers were Ian Waller (Big Wal), Derek Leckenby (Lek), and myself.

By the time The Wailers were born I had left school with one qualification in woodwork, and two bronze medals in Latin American dancing. I genuinely thought that those pieces of paper were all I'd need to face the world. However, it became clear that I was going to need something to fill the gap while I was serving my pop star apprenticeship, so, naturally, I enrolled at a hairdressing college in the centre of Manchester. It had its benefits; firstly, most of the male school leavers were going into mechanics, engineering etc. – manly type jobs, so there was virtually no competition to go into hairdressing. Secondly, I was one of only two males at the hairdressing college. Who needs grease and muck when you can spend your days working with dozens of delightful-smelling girls? Not me, that's for sure.

My school careers officer didn't take me seriously when I told him I was going to be a famous ladies hairdresser, and then a pop star. Then, he was positively rude to me when I suggested that, with my assortment of jobs, I earned as much as he did as a teacher. It was a very brief careers meeting, and I don't think he bothered to take any notes.

So, I'm a trainee hairdresser by day, and a trainee pop star by night. After six months of training, the head of the college was grooming me for hairdressing stardom; I was to become one of his top stylists in his main salon in central Manchester. He even kept me on at the college for an extra three months (at no cost to my mother) so that I would be equipped with all the knowledge I could possibly need. After all the promise, education and preferential treatment...I didn't get the job!

Instead, I ended up working at a salon called Mr. Collins, in Monton village, just outside Manchester. It wasn't quite the salubrious, celebrity salon experience I had been working up to; I was working six days a weeks for a grand total of £4.50, plus £2.50 in tips (on a good week). And the bus trip from home (in East Didsbury) to Monton was a royal pain in the arse…one and a half hours each way (with a change) on over-crowded, over-smoky buses.

One morning on this commute, I remember a beautiful girl taking the only remaining seat on the bus, which just happened to be next to me. As the bus rumbled down the potted streets, I could already feel the curry I'd had the night before making itself known. My stomach wasn't right. After about five more minutes of being bounced around, I released the loudest, most thunderous fart imaginable, prompting everybody on the bus to turn around to discover the source of this wretched sound.

I looked at the girl, who had gone a deep shade of scarlet.

"Don't worry love," I said, at the top of my voice, "they'll all think it was me!"

The rest of the passengers found it funny, but the mortified girl quickly made her way to the lower deck, before leaving the bus at the next stop.

As any other trainee pop star will tell you, a daytime job can really get in the way of one's musical career, particularly as you approach the weekend. This was especially true of hairdressing at the time as the salons opened late on Thursdays and Fridays, meaning that I wouldn't finish work until eight o'clock. And when you have to be at a gig for eight-thirty, that can only mean one thing – Dad to the rescue (again). It led to some pretty hairy drives, but we got through it.

That was until our next-door neighbour told me that he was selling his Lambretta scooter for £25. Convinced that I would kill myself, my mother was against it, but I convinced her that it was important for my independence, and could she please lend me the money to buy it.

It didn't take long before the scooter revealed itself to be utterly unreliable. So, instead of Dad having to pick me up from work and take me to my gigs, he would now have to come out and perform roadside repairs on my Lambretta… almost every night.

Such nocturnal shenanigans, not to mention working two jobs, began to affect my energy levels…I had none. The solution was a caffeine-based tablet called ProPlus. I would arrive at my gig and pop four or five tablets before hitting the stage. But it seemed it was only any good for our first set. Not only did I usually spend our break sleeping somewhere (anywhere), but by the time we started our second set, I was usually flagging so much that one of the lads would have to shout at me to keep up. I was dead on my feet.

This carried on for a few months, and was not only affecting my drumming, but also my daytime job, and I'm certain my parents could see this too. So, I asked my father if he would allow me to turn professional, leaving hairdressing on the backburner. He thought about it for a few days, and finally agreed, although his offer was conditional. His terms were that when he went out to work at eight o'clock in the morning, I would set up my drum kit and practice for eight hours (with a one hour break). The people that built our semi-detached house probably hadn't taken loud drums into their design considerations, so I instantly became very unpopular in the neighbourhood. Worse still, I would sometimes continue when Mum and Dad went to the pub in the evening, but police involvement put paid to that, and I was restricted to daytime sessions.

So, Monday morning arrived, and it would become the day when my life changed…all I had to do was hand in my notice at the salon. It took me a few hours to pluck up the courage to tell Mr Collins that I wanted to be a full-time drummer, but tell him I did, and I also told him that I would give him a few weeks notice, as I felt it was the right thing to do. But what came next nearly floored me; he told me to leave immediately, and ten minutes later I was out of the shop, confidence shattered, and thinking to myself that I must be a really bad hairdresser. I got on my bike, devastated, and headed home to start my new career.

Twenty years later, my father told me what had actually happened that day. Dad had phoned Mr Collins and explained about the late nights, exhaustion and my ambitions, and they made an agreement that if the music didn't work out, I could have my job back. But also, Dad had asked Mr Collins to drop me on the spot, and to let him know what my reaction was. I'm sure the two of them shared a lot of laughter, at my expense. Although, two years after I walked out of the salon, I returned in my Jaguar (which was towing my new boat), doubled parked outside the shop, and popped in to say hello to Mr Collins. I told him "I need a new Jaguar because the ashtrays are full in this one. Anyway, must dash...I'm off to make another number one record." He must have thought I was an idiot.

So I duly committed to practise for eight hours a day – or as much as I could bear, with a lunch break at the Twisted Wheel Club, where Lek was a part-time short order chef, and could normally secure me a free meal. And that's how I became a full-time drummer.

2

Becoming a Hermit

As The Wailers toiled and attempted to perfect their art, on the other side of Manchester, two businessmen, Harvey Lisberg and Charlie Silverman, were trying to elevate a promising young group – Herman & The Hermits – to the dizzying heights of stardom. There was already a buzz about the band, but the rhythm section were proving incapable of providing strong enough backing, so, following a demo recording at Kingsway Studios, London, on 20th March, Mickie Most (who was at the controls) voiced his opinion that the rhythm section wasn't strong enough, it was decided that half of the group would need to be replaced.

As fortune would have it, Harvey Lisberg had attended university with Lek, and was also a regular diner at the Twisted Wheel. Harvey knew that Lek was in a capable band and came up with a proposition that would change both of our lives forever…would the Wailers back Peter Noone, and become the new Hermits?

This great opportunity could easily have been lost in a heartbeat, as Lek had seen Herman & The Hermits play at the Twisted Wheel, and not only did he not think much of their musical skills, on one occasion he even had to show them how to set up their own P.A. system. He was on the verge of telling Harvey to 'stick his offer up his ass', when Harvey took out the group's diary and showed him the bookings the band had for the next six months. Lek later told me that his eyes nearly popped out of his head; they were working seven nights a week, very often doing doubles – which was playing one club, then heading off to play another immediately afterwards. Looking back, there were even occasions when we played three shows in one night. I, of course, said I'd do it…what more could a professional musician desire? A full diary means a full pocket.

But first, there was the small matter of negotiating our way through an audition.

We turned up at the house that Charlie Silverman's father owned, and set up our gear in the basement. After we'd done a couple of warm-up songs, Harvey and Charlie entered the room.

"Right lads," said Harvey, "give us a couple of the songs you do in your show."

I don't recall what we played, but we didn't get the reaction we were expecting, in spite of our youthful hubris, and when Harvey and Charlie left the basement for a chat we thought we'd blown it. So we had a quick conference, and on their return we launched into another staple from our repertoire – Hava Nagila – an old Hebrew song that begins slowly and dramatically, steadily speeding up and building into a frenzy. As we played through the crescendo, I could tell we were on the right track as both men were smiling and infectiously tapping their toes, and seemingly on the brink of breaking into an Ottoman dance routine. When we finished, they applauded and asked us to play the song again, which we dutifully did, safe in the knowledge that we had turned things around. They offered us the job, and on the 1st April, 1964, Lek and I became members of the newly renamed Herman's Hermits (we insisted on changing the name to modernise it and to inform the already large fan-base that there had been a change). Sadly for Big Wal, his father wouldn't let him leave his apprenticeship, so surviving member, Karl Green, switched from guitar to bass, Keith Hopwood remained on rhythm guitar, and Lek and I were enlisted on lead guitar and drums, respectively. This was the line-up that was to make us a household name.

Years later, Alan Wrigley, the ousted bass player, told me that Harvey had paid him off in exchange for not 'beating him up' after his sacking. Alan didn't take it well, and it wasn't long before his misery was confounded. When Peter moved to London, he became friends with a New Musical Express writer called Norrie Drummond. The last time Alan saw Peter was at Euston Station as he was boarding a train back to Manchester. As the train pulled off, Norrie said: "don't worry, Alan…I'll be taking care of Peter from now on."

The man I replaced, Steve Titterington, dealt with his woes by opening a fish and chip shop. Music can be a fickle mistress.

The first big difference I noticed between being a Wailer and being a Hermit was financial; I was now earning about £25 a week, which was a small fortune back then, and not only were we out playing shows six or seven nights a week, but we also had a roadie, Rick Jones. My relationship with Rick got off to the worst possible start. We were playing a show in Aston Palace, Manchester to a room full of almost exclusively girls. Ten minutes before we were due on stage I peered out from the dressing room to check the view, and was flabbergasted to see that my drums were still sat in their cases at the side of the stage. I turned to see Rick sat stage-side, casually smoking a cigarette.

"What the fuck are you playing at?" I enquired. "Why aren't the drums set up?"

"I only work for Peter now," he sneered, before sashaying away to the other side of the stage.

So I had ten frantic minutes putting my kit up in front of a room full of excited girls, with barely a second to spare before the compere announced us. What a dirty trick to play.

On another memorable occasion, we'd just finished a show at the Wigan Empire and, consumed by hunger, made a spontaneous stop at a fish and chip shop. We were recognised by a group of excitable girls, so made a hasty exit with our supper. As we were getting into the van, we saw twelve lads coming towards us…trouble etched across their faces. Lek was last to get into the van, and as he did, one of the lads slammed the door into his back, the force of which caused Lek to drop his pie, chips and gravy onto the pavement. Lek spun around to see a dozen guys in a semi-circle, who had clearly decided that it would be fun to beat up a pop band.

"Pass me that bottle," Lek said, extending his arm into the van without taking his eyes off the aggressors. I passed him a two-litre glass bottle of cider.

"Who the fuck did that? I'll smash your bleedin' head in," he shouted at the group, brandishing the bottle. Now I knew we were in trouble.

In a split second, three of the men were laying into Lek.

"Come on," I shouted to Karl and Keith, who were blocking my escape from the van. Keith comically slipped on the gravy and ended up under the van being kicked by two of the lads. With some help from my foot, Karl flew out of the side door and took out two of the enemy, before being turned on. I jumped out and floored one of them with a sharp punch to the right ear.

Lek was now twenty-odd-feet down the pavement, tightly gripping the head of one of the assailants under his arm, and pounding it relentlessly with the cider bottle. Somehow, the bottle was still intact. Soon enough, one of his cohorts came to his assistance, and managed to disarm Lek. As the man swung the bottle back, I sprinted towards them as quickly as I could in an effort to save my friend. The scene seemed to play in slow motion…frame by frame I could see the arc of the bottle moving ever closer to Lek's head. In a frantic last-ditch move, I threw myself into the air and dropkicked the man, changing the course of the bottle, which missed Lek's head by a fraction of an inch. My victim bounced off a shop window, which seemed to have a similar integrity to the cider bottle.

The two men were dazed enough for me to grab Lek and make our way back to the van, where Keith was still being kicked back underneath every time he attempted to escape. Karl was holding his own against two of the lads, as Peter shouted encouragement from the passenger seat of the van, where he had been sat throughout the entire conflict.

We took a few further swings at the remainder of the mob – I kicked one of them in the balls – just giving us enough time to bundle ourselves into the van. To our utter amazement, Rick hadn't even started the engine.

"For fuck's sake, Rick, get us out of here," I shouted, as I closed the door behind me.

In an anxious moment that was reminiscent of an action film, the sluggish battery in our van vehemently refused to turn over, until the fifth or sixth attempt when it stuttered into life, and we finally had forward motion.

As we left the injured mob behind us, one of the lads picked up the cider bottle, and in an Olympic grade effort, threw it in the direction of our escaping vehicle. It was an almost impossible shot, but it was a perfect throw. The bottle impacted the roof of the van with an almighty explosion, and we drove away with an apple-based foam running down our windows.

"Thanks for your help," I announced to the pair in the front seats, wiping the sweat from my brow and trying to regain my breath.

We were about a mile down the road when Lek had a realisation.

"I've lost my bloody glasses," he said, "we'll have to go back."

Reluctantly, we turned around and were relieved to see that the lads had scraped themselves off the floor and gone, and we were amazed to find Lek's glasses with not a single scratch on them.

As we drove off again, we saw one of the offenders walking down the road, alone.

"Let's get the bastard," somebody shouted.

We gave chase in the van, and no doubt frightened the life out of him, but he got away. It was probably for the best as we could have ended up in a very different kind of trouble…the kind with prison bars.

When I arrived home, mother was waiting up for me.

"Have you been fighting?" she challenged.

"No mum," I lied.

"So why is the sleeve of your jacket hanging off?"

"Ah…" I uttered, looking down at my arm.

I loved that jacket. My mum had recently made it for me, and it was fashioned on the grey Bavarian jackets that The Beatles wore. This had been its first outing.

I confessed that we'd been on the receiving end of an attack in Wigan, but she was glad, of course, that I was okay, and made me a cup of tea. There is no situation when having a cup of tea isn't the perfect remedy.

The next morning I was awoken by excruciating pain, which, under inspection in the mirror, was because of a perfect impression of a size twelve boot in the middle of my chest. It was quite a battle scar.

Later that day we headed off to another show, visiting Barratts music store on the way, where we bought five piano legs to arm us for the next time we were set upon. We never did use them in anger, but they got good use as prodding sticks during episodes of tomfoolery going to and from gigs.

I was somewhat grateful when Rick left our service sometime later…there was no love lost between us.

So here I was in an up-and-coming pop group, earning decent money, and with plenty of work coming in. I recall regularly heading home at seven-thirty in the morning, driving past my father on his way to work. We would acknowledge each other with a flash of our headlights. I would usually get home and have some breakfast, then squeeze in a few hours sleep before heading into town for some lunch and coffee. The rest of our time was spent rehearsing; successful groups had to be tight, fresh sounding, and have a strong repertoire of ever-changing songs, so we made sure we put the hours in.

We would often rehearse at the Plaza Club on Oxford Street in Manchester, where they gave us the room for free so long as we played the lunchtime dance set. Lunchtime gigs were commonplace in the early sixties – it seems strange now to imagine office workers having a bite to eat then going for a dance, all in their lunch hour. By late afternoon we'd be hungry again, so we'd invariably meet at the Wimpy Bar on Oxford Street before heading to the next show. Karl was sleeping with a girl that worked there, so afternoon refreshments were often taken without money changing hands.

I was a little behind the other boys when it came to sexual activity, largely because of my mother's unique brand of sex education; she had told me, in no uncertain terms, that I would catch something horrible and my 'thing' would fall off. It would take the best part of a year before I would take the plunge and 'break my duck'.

A watershed moment for the band occurred on 19th May 1964, when we played a show at the Beachcomber Dungeons in Bolton. In what turned out to be an inspired move, Harvey sent a return airline ticket to record producer, Mickie Most, in an attempt to lure his services. Most, who had already enjoyed chart success with The Animals, turned up and was so impressed that he took us under his wing there and then. He left Harvey with three songs and told us to rehearse them before we would head down to London to record them at the EMI studios in – ironically – Manchester Square. So we headed back to the Plaza to perfect the songs, in between all of our evening commitments.

It didn't take us long to decide which of the songs we liked best, a Goffin/King song entitled 'I'm Into Something Good', performed by Earl Jean & the Cookies.

I had only been inside a recording studio once in my life... Johnny Roadhouse's Music Shop in Manchester, where the walls were so thin you could hear bus bells ringing as they drove past. But this was going to be a proper recording studio where hundreds of hits had been recorded. The session was booked from 10am until noon on Monday, and I was shitting myself.

On the Sunday evening we had a show at a great club in Manchester called Jungfrau Coffee Dance Club, so we made the decision to travel down to London straight after the gig so that we wouldn't be late.

On the 26th July, 1964, we arrived in London at seven o'clock in the morning, tired and hungry, so decided to get a wash and something to eat at Paddington Station. After breakfast we drove to the studio. The morning was warming so quickly that the van began to feel like an oven, so Peter and I opened the back doors, dangled our feet out, and in our exuberance, laughed and joked at all the people going to work. Before long, we were pulled over by a police motorcyclist who explained that if we didn't keep our feet inside the van, they would soon be in a police cell. We thought it best to comply considering the importance of the day, although we couldn't resist sharing a few hand gestures with the policeman from behind the safety of the now closed van door.

By 10am we were at the Kingsway Recording Studio ready to start, and two hours later, both A and B-side (I'm Into Something Good/Your Hand In Mine) were in the can. Recording didn't take long in those days as the studios only had 2-track tape machines (The Beatles famously recorded their first album, Please Please Me, in just a day – ten songs in less than thirteen hours!). The standard process was to record the backing track, and then the vocals would be laid down, before the lead vocal was double-tracked. Aside from our performances, the only other player in this session was bandleader, Roger Webb, who added the piano part to I'm Into Something Good. It was a simple procedure, and it was all over in the blink of an eye.

After the session, Karl and I decided to sunbathe in a park opposite EMI House, while the other boys visited some music shops. It was a private park, so we had to climb over the spiked fence to get in, but we thought it was a worthwhile way to spend a couple of hours before the arranged meeting time of 2pm at the van. It had been a busy few days and Karl and I both fell asleep in the blazing London sunshine, only to be awoken by the van's horn blasting, accompanied by one of the boys shouting; "come on you bastards, hurry up or we'll leave without you!"

We ran to the fence, I, with my brand new leather jacket under my arm, and scaled the spiky perimeter, but my jacket got caught on the top.

"You've got five seconds before we leave," shouted Keith.

With that, I gave my jacket a yank, and we ran as quickly as we could and jumped into the now-moving van. Upon closer inspection, it was apparent that, yet again, I had a jacket with the sleeve hanging off. My annoyance was met with laughter, but this episode marked the last time I was ever late for anything in my life.

As part of our PR push, our management had arranged for us to have some suits made before we had our first photo session. The tailor was a friend of Charlie and Harvey and his name, believe it not, was Abbe Sacks. What a name for a tailor! His son, Michael, had the job of taking the measurement for the suits. Lek was first to be measured.

"What do you play?" asked the tailor.

"Guitar," Lek replied, at which she asked him to stand with an invisible guitar in the same way he would on stage.

She measured him up and asked if anybody else played guitar. Karl and Keith put their hands up and she measures them too, in their stage poses. Peter is next and stands with an invisible microphone as he too is measured.

"You must be the drummer?" she inquired, and tells me to sit on a chair and pretend to play the drums, before writing down my vital statistics.

A couple of weeks later we're having our first professional photo-session, and the photographer gets us to stand in a line. After quizzically looking at me for a while he asks me to straighten my legs.

"My legs are straight," I reply, "it's the trousers that are bent."

By the end of August, 1964, I had been a Hermit for just four months, we'd been under the guidance of Mickie Most for two months, and on the 26th August, we released our first single, I'm Into Something Good (released 7th August on Columbia). On 2nd September we made our debut appearance on Top of the Pops alongside The Zombies, The Honeycombs, Dave Berry, Manfred Mann, The Kinks and Marianne Faithful. Life was moving very fast, but we had no idea what was about to happen...

3

Stardom

On the 24th September 1964, a month after Something Good had been released, I was phoned by Harvey and told that our record was number one in the UK charts. I immediately left the house and walked down our road with the air of a king – my head held high, and a huge smile on my face. Young men were rarely seen in the streets in the daytime back then…if they were, they were either sick or skiving off work. If anybody should ask me, I was an eighteen-year-old professional musician with a number one hit. Of course, nobody did. On 30th September, during a Radio Luxembourg appearance, we received a silver disc for 250,000 sales of our debut single. By the end of this week, sales would reach 370,000.

Overnight, our lives had transformed from 'busy' to 'rollercoaster'.

Bands didn't make videos for their songs in the sixties, so not only were we dashing around the country to make as many TV and radio appearances as we physically could, but we had a tremendous quantity of advance bookings that we had to honour. It's an odd situation when you're number one in the charts but have to play small clubs for just £25, instead of the £500 that our new bookings were worth.

We did one show at the Oasis Club in Manchester where the manager, Tony Stuart, decided not to pay us because he thought we didn't need the money anymore. But the bookings and media appearances flooded in. This made my parents very happy, who regularly invited neighbours around to watch us starring on TV shows. Not every household had a TV set in those days, so it was quite common for friends and neighbours to watch somebody else's set – and having a pop star for a son was the perfect excuse for my proud parents.

23rd October 1964 – NME reports sales of 470,000 for I'm Into Something Good in the UK, and already 250,000 sold in the US — which earned us a gold disc after only two weeks.

After Something Good had spent two weeks at number one, and neared the end of its fifteen-week stint in the charts, it was time to release our second single, so we headed to De Lane Lea Studios in London. Harvey was adamant that he was going to choose our next single to record, and in spite of Mickie's objections, he got his way. He chose another Goffin/King song called Show Me Girl, and when it peaked at only number 19, Harvey had to concede that perhaps Mickie did know more about making hit records than he did.

The press had a field day at our expense - "Herman's Hermits Flash in the Pan", "Herman's Hermits are One Hit

Wonders", and other such headlines, but we were far from done.

Our agent, Danny Betesh (the founder of Kennedy Street Enterprises – one of the biggest and most respected agencies in pop), was keeping us very busy. The remainder of 1964 saw us on a major UK tour with Dusty Springfield, Dave Berry and Brian Poole and the Tremeloes, followed by a six-week run at the Royalty Theatre in Chester starring in the pantomime Dick Whittington. We also returned to the Kingsway Studio on 1st December to complete recordings for our first album, the self-titled Herman's Hermits (which was released the following year).

Before the pantomime run could begin, it was decided that we should make a short PR visit to the States to capitalise on the steady climb that I'm Into Something Good was making in the US charts, and on 10th December we left for our whistle-stop visit. It had been less than a year since the Beatles had made their US TV debut, and American audiences were clearly in the mood to lap up all things British.

Plans were made for us to appear on as many TV and radio shows as humanly possible. We would run into a TV studio, mime to one of our records, then make a mad dash to get to the next studio. The lads had their guitars with them, but all I had was a pair of drumsticks, so I was very much at the mercy of whatever the studios were able to provide for me to play. Sometimes there was no drum kit at all, so I would have to bang on whatever I could find. One studio told me they didn't have a drum kit, but they did have a trombone. I didn't need any encouragement to mime along with a trombone, much to the hilarity of the other boys.

During this stay we recorded Can't You Hear My Heartbeat for the legendary US TV show Shindig! We'd just flown into Los Angeles, and were very tired and jet-lagged, and this was evident in our first three takes of the song. After a while a voice from the control-room asked us to 'put some life into the song', which, we attempted to do on the next run through. Shortly afterwards the show's producer, Jack Good, appeared with a bottle of whisky and some paper cups, and ordered us to take a ten-minute break with the liquor. It did the trick…the next take was far livelier and the recording was used.

In the blink of an eye, it was the 15th of December, and we were back in London's Kingsway Studios recording Wonderful World, the very day after Sam Cooke's murder hit the news.

After a week or so of live shows and TV recordings, we began a six-week run of pantomime at the Royalty, Chester. We had a tremendous amount of fun in Chester. At the first day of rehearsals when we met the twelve dancing girls in the cast, I quickly realised that this was going to be the perfect opportunity to take my final step into manhood. The very next day, in a calculated and devious move, I rented myself a flat about half a mile from the theatre. With a sophisticated bachelor pad, I couldn't possibly fail.

The other four lads were all stopping in a bed and breakfast together, while I had my own place – there was no contest. That was, until I found out that most of the dancers were staying in the same bed and breakfast as the boys. They were shagging themselves to death and I was getting nothing…I couldn't even pull the skin off a rice pudding. (Rumours abounded that by the time we left Chester, there was a little hermit in a proverbial oven).

Feeling dejected that my virginity was intact and the other boys were getting more than they could cope with, I decided to throw a party. I invited the lads and as many of the dancers as I could. Once all the food and drink were devoured, the crowd soon thinned out to the point that the only people left were myself and the least attractive of the dancers. We chatted for a while, but the memory of what my mother said kept jumping to the front of my thoughts, so she eventually left and I was home alone.

I put a record on and fell asleep on the sofa, but I was awoken shortly afterwards by the creaking of the door. I looked up and saw the silhouette of somebody standing in the doorway. I stood up and blinked my drunken eyes in the hope that one of the dancers was still there, but the figure had gone. I looked in the other rooms and the landing, and checked that the door was still locked from the inside, but there was nobody there. Bloody great – I couldn't even pull a ghost.

A couple of days before the pantomime closed, my luck changed. The daughter of the wardrobe mistress turned up to give her mom a hand sorting some costumes. After a while she told me she had something to show me in the wardrobe room, so I, of course obliged. As soon as we entered, she grabbed me and passionately kissed me on the lips. Tonight's the night, I thought to myself. Bollocks to what mother said.

We had sex on some cloth sacks in the corner of the room (I know – very romantic). She was absolutely insatiable…she very nearly destroyed me. The only thing that snapped me out of my post-carnal daze was the sound of the backstage PA system informing us that there were five minutes to curtain. I had to run back to the dressing room and don my sailor outfit for the opening scene. As I was changing, I had a feeling of discomfort between my legs, so I pulled down my pants to reveal an unfamiliar scene. Her voracious appetite had rendered my foreskin inexplicably trapped behind the end of my penis. Damn it…mother was right. Of course, I couldn't tell the other lads because they would naturally have assumed that I'd lost my cherry long before.

By the end of the day's second show, my knob had been rubbing inside my pants, and I was in great pain. In panic, I returned to my flat and held my chap under the cold tap for twenty minutes, and slowly managed to rearrange it back to how it should have been. A few weeks later I asked Karl about safe sex. He said safe sex was not telling the girl your real name and address.

It wasn't just nocturnal shenanigans that make Chester memorable; we also had an awful lot of fun and tomfoolery during the pantomime itself, which for the director, Dennis Chritchley, was a constant challenge to his blood pressure. We would interchange characters on the spur of the moment, put on ridiculous, unrehearsed voices, and sabotage anybody and anything.

Our favourite prank neigh on gave him a nervous breakdown as he shared the Royal Box with the Mayor of Chester. The second half of the show began with the twelve dancers stood in a semicircle, each with two hand-bells. They didn't really know how to play the bells, so they'd simply learnt their parts by counting, and when all of the differently pitched bells are played at the right time, it made a wonderful sound.

However, should the bells be switched around side-stage shortly before curtain, the resulting cacophony is enough to make the listener wish for deafness. The director sprinted from the box, interrupted our childish laughing fit backstage, and gave us an almighty telling off, threatening to cancel the pantomime if we didn't behave. We managed to keep the peace for a couple of days.

Another prank was at the expense of the lead dancer, who happened to be going out with the trumpet player in the house band, who had a clubfoot and a very relaxed approach to hitting the right notes. The opening song of the show involved all of the dancers, and the Hermits dressed as sailors, each of us with a white kitbag. To make the bags look real they were stuffed with newspaper and cardboard, so only weighed a couple of pounds. In the middle of the dance routine, we would hand the bags to the dancers, who in turn would dance off to the wings, leaving us to do some dialogue. One night, Karl put two twenty-eight-pound stage weights in his kitbag. When it came to hand it to the lead dancer, she was, of course, expecting a very light bag, but the bag thumped into the stage with the volume of a cannon. As the other dancers gracefully left the stage, the poor lead dancer was forced to awkwardly drag fifty-six pounds of metal off stage. We got a further reprimand from the director, and during the interval we could hear the trumpet player's clubfoot dragging up the stairs to our dressing room, where he shouted that he was going to take Karl outside for a fight.

"Stick that trumpet up your arse and piss off," Karl shouted back, much to our amusement.

It didn't take long into the pantomime run before we knew how much time we had between our scenes, and a couple of those gaps were long enough for us to nip over the road to the pub for a couple of swift pints. We always made sure we were dressed correctly for our next scene, whether it was as a sailor or a town crier. We got some odd looks from some people, but the landlord had his timing perfected, to the point that our pints would be ready on the bar for us. One of our scenes involved throwing cotton wool snowballs at the dancers. However, one night, it snowed for real outside, so we mustered up a large basket of the real thing. The dancers, the house band, and the first two rows of the audience were all on the receiving end, and, of course, we were once again thoroughly admonished.

The six-week run in Chester would take us into the beginning of February 1965, and it would be four years before we did another pantomime.

1964 stats...
Singles (UK):   I'm Into Something Good (Peak No.1)
                Show Me Girl (Peak No.19)
Singles (US):   I'm Into Something Good (Peak No.13)

4

The USA

With the pantomime in Chester behind us, and after the disappointment of Show Me Girl, we headed back to the studio in February 1965, and with Mickie Most back in charge of the song selection, we recorded an old doo-wop song by The Rays called Silhouettes, which climbed to number three in the charts. It was a very welcome return to the right end of the hit parade. Vic Flick was reputedly brought in for the Silhouettes session, but it was actually Lek that nailed the guitar riff in the first take. The other songs recorded in this session were I'm Henry The Eighth, I Am, The End Of The World, For Your Love, I Gotta Dream On, Don't Try To Hurt Me, I'll Never Dance Again, Tell Me Baby and Mrs. Brown, You've Got A Lovely Daughter.

At the same time, our second US release, Can't You Hear My Heartbeat, had made a strong climb, and reached number two on the Billboard Chart. I'm Into Something Good had already reached number thirteen at the end of 1964, making both songs million sellers. So, a tour of the United States was planned. Bearing in mind I was just eighteen-years-old, to say I was excited would be an understatement.

But for the next couple of months, we continued with the gruelling schedule of TV and live shows in the UK that we'd become accustomed to (including a twenty-one-date tour with Del Shannon), which culminated, on 11th April, with the New Musical Express Poll Winners Concert at Wembley Pool (now Wembley Arena). I remember Paul McCartney popped into our dressing room and wished us well.

Seven nights later, we were back on the other side of the Atlantic…

A brief insight into how the music industry works; when we first arrived in New York the previous December, we were greeted at Kennedy Airport by the press, and some representatives of MGM Records (which was our label in the States). We were driven to Manhattan and taken to the Peppermint Lounge, where hundreds of beautiful people were gathered in our honour, all drinking champagne and eating fabulous food. We needed to be available for so many photo opportunities that we missed out on the incredible looking steak, but we did manage to grab a handful of sandwiches each.

A year later, that party was deducted from our record royalties. For a few sandwiches and a soda each, the bill came to five thousand dollars. Bastards.

In another episode of outrageous profligacy…we were signed up to a New York agency called Premier Talent – one of the largest in the States. The boss, Frank Barsalona, who did a great job booking us for live concerts and TV shows, told us that whenever we were in New York, we would have two Limousines at our disposal. It sounds glamorous, but in reality, they were rather old Cadillacs. We used the Limo's roughly four times during our next tour, only for the agency to deduct $8,000. When questioned over the extortionate charge, they informed us that the limos were at our disposal twenty-four hours a day, seven days a week. Bastards.

Anyway, we were back, and about to begin a major tour as part of Dick Clark's Caravan of Stars, but first we had to play a show in New Jersey that had been booked for some time. Our management tried to get us out of it as our appearance fee had grown substantially since the booking was made, but we were forced, reluctantly, to honour the contract.

The venue was Manville High School, and as soon as we had mounted the stage, the 2,000-strong-crowd surged forward. Police and school officials managed to hold them back long enough for us to play two songs, but the screaming girls eventually overcame the meagre security, and were soon making a grab for anyone they could get their hands on. We hadn't been too thrilled to do the show in the first place, so here was our excuse to abandon the stage, and jump into our waiting cars outside.

The cars took us to Bethlehem, Pennsylvania, where we were lined up to play a far more lucrative show. This show took place at the Bandstand, Notre Dame High School, and, incredibly, virtually the same thing happened. Except this time, we were halfway through the first song when, due to the frantic push of fans, the middle of the stage collapsed. We ended up in a pile on the floor with a couple of thousand crazed teenagers about to mob us. They managed to plunder almost everything on stage as souvenirs, but we ran away to the safety of our dressing room, and that, ladies and gentlemen, was the shortest show I've ever performed in my long career.

On 22nd April, prior to a show at the Memorial Auditorium, Dallas, Texas, we visited the Dallas Book Depository (very eerie), went swimming at the Holiday Inn, before attempting an appearance at the local radio station, KBOX. But 6,000 fans blocked the way and the radio station hadn't hired security, so that was the end of that.

It is worth noting that on 24th April 1965, the top three positions in the US charts were occupied by bands from Manchester – Wayne Fontana & The Mindbenders were number one with Game Of Love, Herman's Hermits at number two with Mrs. Brown, You've Got A lovely Daughter, and Freddie & The Dreamers at number three with I'm Telling You Now.

On the 30th April 1965, we began our first proper US tour, as part of Dick Clark's Caravan of Stars. Dick Clark's Caravan was a popular roadshow that featured the most popular singers and groups of the day, and had started life back in 1959 with the likes of Buddy Holly, Chubby Checker and Chuck Berry heading the bill. For this tour we were joined by; Bobby Vee, Little Anthony, Freddie Cannon, Brenda Holloway, The Hondells, Round Robin, Raparata & The Delrons, The Detergents, The Ikettes, and Billy Stewart.

The transportation was beyond belief. It was a regular Greyhound bus with forty-eight seats, which just happened to be the same number of people on the tour. Not a caravan in sight. To make matters worse, every other night was a travel night, so you were lucky to sleep in a real bed more than three times a week.

It gets worse – there was no air conditioning on the bus and the toilet kept backing up which, combined with the smell of body odour was horrendous.

It gets worse – occasionally you would pull the short straw and have to sit next to Billy Stewart (who weighed at least twenty-five stone), so half a seat was the best you could hope for.

It gets worse – one day, as we were about to pull out of a motel, Round Robin boarded the bus and pulled out a revolver and started shouting obscenities at Billy Stewart, who was sat at the back of the bus with Round Robin's girlfriend. So Billy, too, pulls out a revolver and starts waving it around. It eventually calmed down, but the forty-six people sat between the two gunslingers all required fresh underwear.

At the first available moment we made a call to the Dick Clark Organisation and told them in no uncertain terms that we would not travel this way. The next day we were travelling in a station wagon with a driver. It was just as cramped, but the likelihood of being shot was considerably reduced.

Before this tour had started, we were some distance down the bill. This was because British acts had never featured in the Caravan before, so this was fine with us. However, on the second day of the tour (1st May 1965), Mrs. Brown You've Got A Lovely Daughter hit number one on the Billboard charts, and we were instantly propelled to the headline slot, although we were still on the same money. (The same song also rose to number one in Canada, South Africa, New Zealand and Australia.) On this very same day, the show rolled into the Convention Hall, Philadelphia, where the local agent had also booked the Rolling Stones (as well as the Caravan of Stars line-up). This led to a mild stand-off between Harvey Lisberg and Andrew Oldham (the Stones' manager), but it was eventually agreed that we would close the Dick Clark section of the show, and the Rolling Stones we take to the stage forty-five minutes later.

After a while, the clamour for this fresh, new British band, with their exaggerated English accents, all became too much for the screaming fans that greeted us at every town and city. One afternoon, we were relaxing around a hotel pool when one of our agents and our road manager – a certain Dave Lee Travis – told us that we had to remain inside the hotel, where we were corralled into one room and guarded by security around the clock. Our misery was confounded by the fact that, aside from Lek, we were all too young to legally buy alcohol in the States. That didn't stop Lek ordering a few triple vodkas which, once back in our room, would be poured into our legally purchased orange juices.

On 21st May, Victory Stadium, Roanoke, Virginia, was poised for the biggest night in their history with 15,000 tickets sold for the show, but after hours and hours of rainfall the show had to be cancelled. An appearance was rescheduled for 13th June, but without the rest of the Caravan of Stars.

On 1st June, the tour headed north and over the border into Canada for a couple of dates, before crossing back over to the States for a Herman's Hermits show at Exposition Hall, Chicago, where we somehow managed to draw a much bigger crowd than US president, Lyndon B. Johnson, who was giving a speech in the same building. (N.B. We were later invited to perform at the Whitehouse on 2nd July, in honour of President Johnson's daughter, Lucy, but the date conflicted with a tour of Scotland, so we had to decline.)

On the 6th June we made our first appearance on the legendary Ed Sullivan Show, on which we performed Mrs. Brown You've Got A Lovely Daughter, I'm Henry VIII, I Am, and Wonderful World. The Ed Sullivan Show was one of the most popular TV shows of the sixties, and our first performance on the show was somewhat nerve-wracking, as we knew that virtually all of America would be gathered by their TV sets. During rehearsals there was an incident that very nearly caused a strike. The studio electricians had a very strong union, and if you weren't in that union you weren't allowed to touch anything electrical – including guitar amplifiers.

We were given instruction to move to our marks on the studio floor, and Lek instinctively plugged his guitar into his amplifier.

"You can't do that," said one of the electricians, unplugging his cable.

"What do you mean...I can't do that?" queried Lek, plugging his guitar back in.

55

The electrician intervened again and told him that he couldn't plug his guitar into his amp.

"How the fuck can I play the song without plugging my guitar into the amp?" Lek remonstrated, pushing the cable in once again.

The electrician walked off the set muttering: "god-damn-limeys…" before all the studio lights went out, and the studio manager told us to wait in our dressing room until further notice. Shortly afterwards, he came in and told us that we weren't allowed to plug anything in, as it was an electrician's job. We sighed and agreed, and went back to the studio to try again.

It was time for Lek to have some fun, and to highlight the ridiculousness of the situation. Lek's amp had six different inputs, so, a variety of sounds was possible. After the electrician had duly plugged him into one of the inputs, Lek played a few chords before telling the electrician to try another input. This went on for some minutes until he was vaguely satisfied. He then asked the electrician to add some middle to the sound.

"What's middle?" he asked.

"Try a combination of treble and bass," he replied, before calling over the studio manager.

"How the fuck can these guys be in charge of something they don't understand? We'll be here all day," he complained to the manager.

The lights went out again.

After a couple of minutes, the studio manager returned and conceded that plugging in and changing the sound would be the responsibility of the musicians. Common sense had prevailed.

In spite of a perhaps enviable amount of travel, when you're on rollercoaster tours, such as we were, you don't often get to see much, so it was a pleasure to spend a couple of days off in New York City. There were a few inevitable business meetings, but we did manage to visit the Empire State Building and spend some time in Central Park.

After a month back in the UK doing the regular carousel of shows and TV and radio appearances, we returned to the States mid-July. On the 18th July we were scheduled to tape an appearance on the Danny Kaye Show, but it was postponed, so instead we fly to Chicago, arriving at 4am, only to find that Peter's luggage has been lost. He was already feeling sorry for himself after a tooth extraction, so another flight onto Los Angeles did little to raise his spirits. The next morning, we arrived at MGM Studios in L.A. (to film When The Boys Meet The Girls) at 6:30am, only to be greeted by five thousand fans. Sometimes you just want a quiet room

After a few days of filming in ridiculous heat, we began the next leg of our US tour, this time supported by Wayne Fontana & The Mindbenders, Sam The Sham And The Pharaohs, Freddie Cannon, and other local artistes. Each time we started a new tour, I would have to go to Manny's Music Store on W48th Street in New York to get another drum kit because, along with a variety of amplifiers, guitars and microphones, they kept going missing from our agency lock-up. It turned out that Bob Levine, who was running our fan club, was selling the equipment between tours. This tour was the usual mix of mayhem, fun and over exuberant crowds. At an after-show party in Birmingham, Alabama, we celebrated Karl's eighteenth birthday as police held back 5,000 fans in the hotel foyer. That was fairly typical.

On the 1st August, prior to performing at the Municipal Auditorium in New Orleans, we, and Wayne Fontana & the Mindbenders, were fortunate enough to receive keys of the city and honorary citizenship, before enjoying a performance by music legends B.B. King and Clarence 'Frogman' Henry.

On the 12th and 13th August, we were back in New York to rehearse and tape, respectively, an appearance on the Danny Kaye Show. I can't remember much about this recording other than Danny asking Peter a lot of dumb questions, and getting a lot of dumb replies.

The tour eventually concluded on 15th August at the Honolulu International Centre in Hawaii. Exactly a week before, thanks to our appearance on the Ed Sullivan Show, I'm Henry The VIII, I Am had hit the US Billboard chart 'with a bullet', which means it entered the charts at number one. At that point it was the fastest-selling single in US history, in spite of never being released in the UK. 1965 was shaping into a very good year for us, and we were even out-selling The Beatles, at the height of Beatlemania, in the States.

We were due to fly back to the UK on 17th August when something extraordinary happened. Word got to us that Elvis Presley, who was filming Paradise Hawaiian Style nearby, wanted to meet us. Much to their regret, Karl, Lek and Keith took the scheduled trip, but Peter and I managed to rearrange our flights to twenty-four hours later. Peter, Harvey and I arrived on the set at the Hanalei Plantation Resort in Kaui just in time to see Elvis spearheading a throng of Harley Davidsons into the set. Here was the most famous singer in the world – right in front of us – casually climbing down from his motorbike. Not a hair on his head was out of place as he approached us. It turned out he'd bought the Harley Davidsons for his friends, which, by all accounts was typical of his generosity.

We spent a couple of hours with The King and were struck by his warmth and friendliness. We talked about our tour of the US, the film he was making, and more. He seemed a little bemused at how five skinny young lads from Manchester had achieved such fame, and he seemed to want to know our secret. Colonel Tom Parker was very protective of him, and promoted a lot of caution in the questions he was permitted to answer, and only allowed their official photographer to take pictures. But pictures he took, and I'm very proud and grateful that the meeting was documented, as it really was the encounter of a lifetime – 18th August 1965, the day I met Elvis Presley, the king of rock and roll.

He invited us to a party on that evening, but sadly we had to fly home to appear on Top Of The Pops on Thursday 19th August (for the single Just A Little Bit Better). If only we could have used a promotional film for that episode, like the Beatles did. (N.B. This episode was presented by Jimmy Savile, and featured an appearance by Jonathan King – if only we knew then what we know now.)

1965 also saw our first movie appearance in a film anthology called Pop Gear (US title: Go Go Mania), which

59

documented the British invasion of late 1964, which was followed by Herman's Hermits making a cameo appearance in the Connie Francis movie, When The Boys Meet The Girls, which was released in October of 1965.

The remainder of the year was spent making numerous TV appearances, another US tour and filming commitments, a UK tour with Wayne Fontana, The Fortunes, and Billy Fury, a tour of Sweden and Denmark with The Hollies, and a tour of Ireland.

By the end of 1965 we'd sold over 10 million records in the USA in just eight months, and we thoroughly deserved our three-week holiday.

1965 stats...

Singles (UK): Silhouettes (Peak No.3)
Wonderful World (Peak No.7)
Just A Little Bit Better (Peak No.15)
A Must To Avoid (Peak No.6)

Albums (UK): Herman's Hermits (Peak No.16)

Singles (US): Can't You Hear My Heartbeat (Peak No.2)
Silhouettes (Peak No.5)
Mrs. Brown, You've Got A Lovely Daughter (Peak No.1)
Wonderful World (Peak No.4)
I'm Henry VIII, I Am (Peak No.1)
Just A Little Bit Better (Peak No.7)

                    A Must To Avoid (Peak No.8)

Albums (US):   Introducing Herman's Hermits (Peak No.2)
                     Herman's Hermits On Tour (Peak No.2)
                     The Best Of Herman's Hermits (Peak No.5)

5

1966 and all that

January of 1966 saw us undertake our first tour of Australia, billing with a certain Tom Jones, who had hit the big time at about the same time as us. The tour featured two shows a day, with Herman's Hermits closing the afternoon show, and Tom closing the evening show. Often, after shows, we would go to various music clubs, where Tom would always end up on stage singing – he couldn't resist it. Tom got some great publicity when his trousers split on stage one night, a stunt that had severely backfired for PJ Proby just twelve months before.

During that tour, A Must To Avoid (which Peter often referred to as A Muscular Boy) hit number six in the UK, and number eight in the US, becoming another million seller.

It's interesting to note that on 20th January, Top of the Pops was broadcast from London for the first time ever, having been recorded and broadcast from Manchester since its first show on 1st January 1964. We appeared in this show on a recorded performance by virtue of us being on the other side of the world.

In February, on our way back to the USA, we became only the third western act to tour Japan. The tour started badly and with an almost empty auditorium because one of the two western acts that had preceded us, The Animals, had led Japanese parents to believe that all rock and roll bands were as rude and badly behaved as they were, and as a result their children were forbidden to see us. It took a clean-cut and politely conducted TV interview the next morning to convince people that we weren't the same as them…the remaining shows sold out, and it's felt that we were good ambassadors to rock music during our stay there.

On the way home from the Far East we made short stops in Los Angeles and New York, where we received a gold disc for our album The Best Of Herman's Hermits. Amusingly, when we returned to the UK on the 23rd February, the gold disc was confiscated by customs at Manchester Airport because we refused to pay duty on it. Harvey was furious, but we were more interested in the short break we were about to enjoy.

After our little holiday we embarked upon a short tour of Finland, and a somewhat longer UK package tour with Dave Berry and a number of other acts. Then, on 1st May we were back at Wembley Empire Pool for another NME poll-winners concert. Farcically, Peter missed his cue because he was backstage talking to John Lennon. When Lennon heard the opening bars of A Must to Avoid, he said to Peter: "Isn't that your song?"…at which, Peter sprinted onto the stage and joined us halfway through the first line.

The remainder of the spring was taken up by tours of the Philippines, Singapore, Hong Kong and Malaysia, followed by a host of dates, recordings and pressers in the UK and Europe. I've lost track of how many times we've toured the USA, but on 27th June we were back at JFK in ninety-nine-degree heat, ready to go again, this time with support provided by The Animals, another British group who had hit the top of the American charts with the now legendary House Of The Rising Sun. They were a great rhythm and blues band, but their music wasn't really suited to the fans that were turning up for Herman's Hermits concerts. Nevertheless, they were a wild bunch of lads, and we had fun on the road with them, often ending in some legendary water fights.

One night, while staying in a very grand hotel in Baltimore, we had a mammoth water fight that lasted hours, and was only noticed by the hotel manager when water began to leak through the floor into the rooms of other guests. I remember the corridors had marble floors which, when covered in water made a fabulous slide. If you picked up enough speed you could slide the entire length of the corridor, bucket of iced water in hand, and through the door at the end, preferably drowning an Animal or two in the process, or sometimes an unsuspecting hotel guest. We didn't care.

Also on this particular evening, Peter threw a bucket of water with cigarette ends in over Karl. This was deemed to be against the rules, so Karl chased Peter down the corridor and shot him repeatedly in his behind with a BB gun. The sound of Peter shouting "the bastard shot me in the ass" echoed around the corridors. It stung for days. The next morning at checkout, as happened most mornings, the tour manager had to pay for the damage.

We also played a lot of poker with The Animals, as Chas Chandler, their bass guitarist, was a keen player. One day, our plane (a knackered old Martin 202A twin engine airplane) was making its final approach to our destination when the flight engineer interrupted an intense game of poker to tell us to move away from the table and secure ourselves in our seats.

"Bollock's man," barked Chas in his broad Newcastle accent, "we've got over three hundred fucking dollars in the pot. No way man." The flight attendant returned to the cockpit, tutting.

The plane landed okay, but when the pilot put the engines into reverse thrust, one of the engines burst into flames. Now, we all knew that this engine had a habit of setting on fire at every landing, but Harvey Lisberg, who was 'enjoying' his first flight on this particular plane, did not. He jumped out of his seat, clearing the person sat next to him, and ran down the aisle shouting that we were all going to die. We let him panic for a while until our drunken laughter got the better of us, and we gave him a round of applause for his efforts.

Also on that tour were an American group called The Three And A Half, so named because of their diminutive drummer. I had just started a sponsorship/endorsement deal with Slingerland Drums and I always chose the biggest set of drums I could get my hands on, and, as a result, the drummer from The Three And A Half couldn't be seen. They should have changed their name to The Three for that tour.

The tour had actually opened in Honolulu, following which we had three very welcome days off, so I decided to do what virtually everybody in Hawaii was doing, and try my hand at surfing. In my usual way, I hadn't sought any advice or instruction on how to do it, but I'd watched plenty of other people do it, and it looked pretty easy. The only board available to rent was ten foot long. The guy who rented it to me asked if I wanted some wax.

"What's the wax for?" I asked.

"It stops you sliding off," he replied.

"You'd better give me a couple of blocks," I confirmed.

He gave me one block and told me to rub it on the top of the board, which I did, looking every bit the surfer. I looked even more the part as I carried my board to the water's edge, but that was where the similarity ended. I pushed the board out across the water, jumped onto it, and immediately fell off the other side. It was a great start. So I pushed my board out further, heading for what looked like small breakers, and rolled onto the board belly-down. The first wave, about three feet high, rolled over me, went in my eyes, ears and nose, and propelled me most of the way back to the shore. It was time to channel my inner Beach Boy and push the board out beyond the breakers, where the water was flatter and the going was easier. After my fourth attempt, I made it, and eventually managed to hoist myself onto my knees like the real surfers were doing.

Things were going well until I was suddenly faced with a six feet wall of fast-moving water, which promptly took me off my board in spite of me using what I thought was expert technique. After being sucked beneath the offending wave, I finally resurfaced to see that it had taken my board all the way back to the shore, and it took me about ten minutes to be reunited with it. It was during the swim back that I considered how useful it would be to have a leash that connects your foot to the surfboard, but that wouldn't be invented for another five years.

I'm sure the Pacific Ocean had dropped a couple of inches courtesy of the water I had taken in, but I'm not one to give in, so back in I went again. After many more attempts I found myself in a good position with another large wave approaching, and I was floating alongside somebody who really looked like he knew what he was doing. As the wave drew nearer, he started to paddle, so I also started to paddle. Once he'd picked up some speed he stood up, so I also stood up. Admittedly it wasn't for long, but for those two seconds I was on my feet, I felt like the very embodiment of Brian Wilson. Then the wave hit me, and I didn't even have time to shout 'wipeout' before I was deep beneath the surface struggling for breath. I opened my eyes and could see the surface, so pushed myself up off the ocean floor with all my might. The good news was that I was propelling myself closer to the shore with every attempt, and I crawled out of the sea to an ironic round of applause from some real surfers. That was enough for me for one day, and I staggered back to my hotel, leaving my board where it had washed up on the beach.

The next morning, I woke up feeling like I'd gone the distance with Muhammad Ali – I had a nasty case of what they call 'surfer's bumps. Later that day, Karl, Peter and I went for a swim, and seeing a sandbank about one hundred yards out, decided to swim to it. We had no trouble reaching it, and spent some time lounging in the sun on our own private island. However, after twenty minutes or so, the bank started to get smaller as the tide came in, so it was decided that we should swim back and enjoy some beers in the hotel. All three of us went in the water at the same time, but only two of us made it to the beach. Karl and I looked at each other, before scoured the area for Peter, who had been taken away from the beach in a riptide. It took all our strength to get back to the diminishing sandbank, but we made it. Once there, out of breath, we could see Peter being pulled this way and that by the tide. Karl looked at me.

"What do you think, Baz?" he asked.

I considered how badly Peter treated us, and what a prat he was.

"I dunno," I replied, "what do you think?"

But we realised that he was going to drown if we didn't do something quickly, so in we went. Exhausted, we swam out to him, grabbed him between us, and slowly pulled him back to shore. I realised later that I'd been in the water in Hawaii twice, and nearly drowned on both occasions.

Prior to the Canadian stretch of the tour, The Animals had been warned by the tour manager about taking drugs into Canada, as their customs officers were somewhat officious, and it would result in everybody on the tour being arrested, and the plane impounded. Ten minutes before we were due to land in Toronto, I went to the toilet at the back of the plane, only to find Chas and Eric Burdon sat at the table with a lump of dope the size of a house brick. They were breaking up the block into smaller pieces, and putting the chunks into a wooden coffee grinder. Eric was turning the handle and Chas laughed as he placed the resulting grain into small bags.

"What are you doing? You must be mad," I proclaimed, but this only made them both laugh more.

The tour manager came back to investigate the commotion, and asked them how much stuff they had. "Four or five bricks worth," replied Chas, proudly.

It was discussed that because it was a privately chartered flight, perhaps we would be taxied to a quiet part of the airport and allowed to slip through. No. As we came to a standstill, the plane was surrounded by the Canadian National Guard, some of them with machine guns, some with sniffer dogs. We had approximately one minute before they would be up the steps and into our mobile drug den.

"Right, you fuckers," shouted our tour manager, "get rid of all that shit and make it bloody quick!"

Chas, Eric and the rest of The Animals started to eat the drugs, as the tour manager threw the rest down the chemical toilet. Just at the last flush of the toilet, the back door burst open, and customs officers and sniffer dogs filled the plane.

"Everybody remain in your seats," shouted one of the officers, "we have reason to believe there are drugs on this plane."

"What on earth are you on about," replied our tour manager, "this is a Herman's Hermits tour. They don't even drink or smoke, let alone take drugs," he lied.

69

After a long search, they gave up and left, leaving Eric and Chas dribbling in the corner. They were stoned for several days.

It was also during this tour that Lek came to me with a badly sunburnt neck, and asked if I had anything that might soothe it. I went back to my room and had a rummage through my bathroom bag and returned with what Lek thought was after-sun cream. I told him to hold out his hand while I squeezed the cream into his palm. As soon as he started to rub the cream into his neck, I ran away from him as quickly as I could.

"What the hell are you doing?" he shouted after me.

"You'll find out in a few seconds," I replied, still running.

A few seconds later I heard his bloodcurdling screams as the Deep Heat started to infiltrate his nerve endings. He tried to give chase but my head start was too good. Never the less, I kept a healthy distance from him for a few days.

Our Autumn US tour, with The Hollies, was a far more sedate affair…they were a nice group and very much kept themselves to themselves. My enduring memory is of poor Bobby Elliott, The Hollies drummer, turning green with sickness every time we got into the plane. Our plane (this one was an old DC3) was such a wreck it couldn't travel higher than twenty thousand feet, which meant flights were very bumpy. Combined with faulty air-conditioning, it made for uncomfortable flying.

We had three different planes during the sixties for our US tours, all of which had 'Herman's Hermits' emblazoned in huge letters down the side, but none of which lasted very long.

All three planes had been well used by various corporations, and were handed down to us after their scheduled service, so it's unsurprising that we had a variety of incidents. Knowing how many pop stars died in aircraft accidents in the fifties and sixties, I'm somewhat grateful to still be here.

All through the sixties we, or rather our legal team, were involved in court battles over performance royalties. These disputes rumbled on until 1972, and still didn't end very satisfactorily. Point in case: in August 1966, Billboard Magazine calculated that Herman's Hermits had grossed $680,000 from that year's summer tour. How much of that did we see? Not very much.

Unsurprisingly that wasn't the last tour of the States that year…there were two more (the second one with support from The Hollies). There was also a tour of Iceland, a string of UK dates, visits to Germany and Holland, and untold recording sessions.

As we had done the previous year, we, and our producer, Mickie, continued to strive for a more interesting roster of songs than some bands released. We managed to release Dandy, by Ray Davies, before even the Kinks version had come out, and we also recorded three songs by young songwriter, Graham Gouldman (later the driving force behind 10cc) – Listen People, No Milk Today, and East West. No Milk Today had originally been written for The Hollies, but they turned it down. It became the first recording we'd made with string orchestrations, with the chimes being played by John Paul Jones, who later became the bass player with Led

Zeppelin (JPJ also joined us as keyboard player for a tour of Germany in 1968).

Graham's was a remarkable story; writing songs in the back of the gentleman's outfitters where he worked, he had written For Your love (The Yardbirds), Bus Stop (The Hollies), and Pamela Pamela (Wayne Fontana) by the time he was nineteen-years-old…quite a start to an incredible career.

What a year 1966 had been. We had reinforced the efforts of the year before and become truly global stars, had numerous million sellers, and outsold the Beatles in the States. We'd only had a few days off throughout the whole year, but it had been worth it.

1966 stats…

Singles (UK): You Won't Be Leaving (Peak No.20)
This Door Swings Both Ways (Peak No.18)
No Milk Today (Peak No.7)
East West (Peak No.33)

Singles (US): Listen People (Peak No. 3)
Leaning On The Lamp Post (Peak No. 9)
This Door Swings Both Ways (Peak No. 12)
Dandy (Peak No. 5)
No Milk Today (Peak No. 35)
East West (Peak No. 27)

Albums (US): When The Boys Meet The Girls

(Peak No. 61)
Hold On! (Peak No. 14)
Both Sides Of Herman's Hermits
(Peak No. 48)
The Best Of Herman's Hermits, Vol. 2
(Peak No. 20)

6

The Endless Road

The US tour with The Hollies continued into 1967, and New Year's Day found is in a very chilly Duluth, Minnesota. The only reason I can be certain of this is down to the diligence and enthusiasm of a lifelong fan, and that wonderful resource we call 'the internet'.

We were so relentlessly busy, particularly during this period of our career, that to recall the specific events of over fifty years ago would be practically impossible. As with anybody's recollections of their own life, the highs and the lows are indelibly imprinted on my mind…the many episodes that made us laugh like drains, run in fear, or drunkenly escapade are perfectly intact. But precise details are not.

So this is the perfect opportunity to tip my cap to Olaf Øwre. Olaf is a writer and rock music archivist from Finnsnes, Norway, and it is because of his unrelenting curiosity and fastidious sense of investigation that I am able to pinpoint exactly where I was, what I was doing, and who I was with, on virtually any day of my lengthy career.

Olaf's interest in Herman's Hermits began in the mid-sixties when he was just twelve-years-old. We were as big in Scandinavia as we were everywhere else, so it would be no surprise that a legion of fresh, enthused young fans would emerge. But Olaf was different.... Olaf was, and is, a super-fan! Once he could afford his first record player, his zest and passion for the Hermits knew no boundaries as he strived to collect every release and every morsel of merchandising and information that he could get his hands on. His Herman's Hermits collection now has a count of many thousands of singles, EPs, albums and CDs, with rarities from such places as Angola, Bolivia, Nigeria, India, Pakistan, Malaysia, Turkey, The Philippines, Saudi Arabia, United Arab Republic (now Egypt) and Zimbabwe, most of which I've never even seen!

Even when Peter left the band to pursue a solo career in 1971, Olaf loved the new direction we'd taken, and counts some of those early seventy's releases amongst his favourites. Then after the US revival tour in 1973, he didn't hear much about the band. After the hits stopped coming, the music press seemed to lose interest. So after a while he decided to write to RCA Records, Melody Maker and Strawberry Studios, Stockport — requesting information about the current whereabouts of his favourite band, Herman's Hermits. Melody Maker published his letter in their Any Questions? column in 1975, and Strawberry Studios kindly forwarded his letter to Lek. He was delighted to receive a personal letter from Lek, in May 1976, with updates about the band's post-Noone singles on the Private Stock, Buddah and Roulette labels. Lek also gave him the address to our agent, Ray Reneri, in New York, who kept Olaf posted on US tour dates and sent publicity photos and promo flyers on a regular basis for many years to come.

With the band touring mostly in the US and Canada in the late 70s, Olaf didn't get to see Herman's Hermits live in concert until 1982 at a club called Studio 26 in Oslo, Norway. Having corresponded with Lek and Ray Reneri for many years, he says it was like a dream come true to finally meet us, and to see the band in concert for the first time. We became good friends after that, and he still has all the letters that he shared with Lek and myself in the ensuing years, as well as having visited all of our family homes.

Olaf tells me that he soon saw the importance of sharing some of the information he had gathered about the band with other fans and collectors, so he tried his hand at writing a number of articles on Herman's Hermits as well as other more obscure groups that emerged on the Manchester music scene in the sixties and seventies, most of which were published in music papers and magazines in the US, UK, France and Scandinavia, then on a number of websites in more recent years.

So, it is by virtue of the comprehensive chronicle that Olaf has compiled that I can say with certainty that I spent 1st January 1967 in Duluth, MN, and it is because of the infinite complexity of the World Wide Web that I can report with confidence that the temperature was about -7C. So it is with boundless gratitude that I say thank you, Olaf, and thank you, Sir Tim Berners Lee, for making this journey easier than it would have been.

We travelled back from a freezing United States to film a TV segment in Brussels, where we had to lip-sync whilst on ice. I was struggling to remember what warmth was! Following Belgium was a series of shows and TV appearances across Scandinavia and the Netherlands, before returning to the US to appear on the Dean Martin Show for our first and only appearance (aired on 30th March), in which we got to sing 'Mares Eat Oats' with the host, with yours truly slapping a pair of drum sticks in his hands. What a nice fellow and a pleasure to work with he was. We filmed the show in L.A., taking a whole day. Dean Martin didn't actually show up during the rehearsals but arrived about an hour before the filming of the show. He used cue cards to read his lines and ad-libbed a lot during the sketches with his guests. He always had a glass of what looked like Bourbon in his hand when he was off camera, and after the show we went to his dressing room for a chat and to see if he might share some of his liquor with us. I can confirm that he did share it, and I got shit-faced in a matter of minutes, unaccustomed as I was to drinking with the big boys. After getting drunk with Dean Martin, I got a lift back to the Beverly Hills Hilton with Donna Douglas, who played the daughter in The Beverly Hillbillies, and was also a guest on the Dean Martin show with us. I invited her back to my room, but she declined.

I don't need archives or the Internet to remember what we did in early April 1967, as we were granted a holiday, the first proper one after three years of constant traveling and performing.

Throughout May and June, we spent our time between Shepperton Film Studios and De Lane Lea Recording Studios as we filmed and recorded the soundtrack for our last feature film, Mrs. Brown, You've Got A Lovely Daughter. If Hold On! was a frolicking glossy snapshot of America at the time, Mrs. Brown was the very embodiment of the swinging sixties in London. As the poster tagline said: "you've got to sing... swing...and do your own thing...and no one does it better in merry young London than Herman's Hermits!"

When filming started, we were stopping at a pub called The Ship Inn, in Sunbury on Thames, but we got thrown out after two weeks for being too noisy. Keith Hopwood and I then hired a boat for a week, before we all moved into the Warren Lodge Hotel, also in Sunbury on Thames. It was quite an expensive hotel, and we partied every night, inviting our showbiz buddies and friends from back home to accumulate an enormous bar and restaurant bill. In three weeks, we were informed that we'd spent nearly £30,000. The filming side was a little dull - we had to be on set at 7:30 every morning and there was a lot of waiting around. Location filming was a lot more fun, like the day we got to sing and dance around Covent Garden dressed as barrow boys. The film was set to be Sandie Shaw's film debut, but she pulled out before production began.

The remainder of 1967 was spent touring in what might be considered a rather peculiar matchup...a North American tour supported by The Who. Although huge in the UK (they had already scored seven top ten hits and two hit albums), The Who were yet to break into the top twenty of the US

Billboard charts, so, difference of genre aside, they opened for us on a gruelling three-month tour of the USA and Canada. To complete the mismatch, also on the tour were The Blue Magoos, puzzling our teenage audiences with their experimental psychedelic rock, and their stage suits that lit up. An incongruous mixture of genres it may have been, but this tour marked the most hilarious, wild and memorable episodes of my life.

For this particular tour, our unreliable hand-me-down aircraft was a four engine DC6, and believe me, it needed all four engines to get off the ground. On the first day of the tour, we all gathered at the airport to try to work out how all of the gear would be loaded onto the plane. Just as the flight engineer was telling us we'd be lucky to get everything into the aircraft, a truck rolled up with three Jewish-Italian guys who would be selling programmes on the tour. We'd made a deal with them that they could sell our programmes as long as they paid for them up front, which meant it took the hassle off us, and it meant they couldn't rip us off. But these guys were pro's who'd been selling merchandise for years, and they turned out to be pretty decent poker players too.

Despite verbal reservations from the flight engineer, we eventually got all of the equipment and a couple of tonnes of programmes loaded up. Once we'd got clearance to take off, the pilot applied as much thrust as was possible, and the reluctant aeroplane slowly made its way down the runway. After an age of painfully slow acceleration, we could see through the open cockpit doors that the end of the runway was rapidly approaching – we had passed the point of no return and the plane would either have to go up, or across a busy highway. Fear was etched onto all of our faces. We just managed to become airborne before it was too late, after clipping some trees at the end of the runway. When we reached our destination, I noticed that there was still some foliage tangled in the wheels, shook my head, and walked away with equal measures of gratitude and dread. After the first show, the pilot told me that he was shitting himself too, and suggested to the programme sellers that they should travel by road should they wish to see the end of the tour. Years later, Pete Townshend said in interview 'I never regarded myself as a person afraid of travelling by air, but when we did the Herman's Hermits tour in an old charter plane, I wrote so many songs about plane crashes, it was incredible.'

It still seems very strange to me that The Who, still one of the biggest names in rock – global giants – only ever had one US top ten hit, and somehow never troubled the top spot in the UK. They were very easy to get on with, and I have to say that I've never met four such contrasting characters in the same group. John Entwistle may have been one of the best bass players in the world, but he was also one of the quietest, introvert people I've ever met. Conversely, Pete Townshend was an extrovert, on and off the stage. Roger Daltrey was the only member of The Who that resembled anything close to normal. Keith Moon was just Keith Moon – untamed, electric, unpredictable, unique…wonderful.

One of the many aspects that perhaps made The Who inappropriate for our enthusiastic, yet tender young audience was Pete Townshend's favourite new hobby of smashing the absolute bejesus out of his guitar at the end of each show. He always reserved this honour for a solid-bodied guitar, which he would throw high above the stage and attempt to land it body first, so that the neck wouldn't break. He sometimes got it wrong, but usually the instrument wasn't so badly damaged that his roadie couldn't rebuild it in time for the next show. One night, a lad backstage asked Pete if he wouldn't mind smashing his guitar to bits at the end of the show, to which Pete said he'd be happy to oblige. He didn't let the young man down; he threw the guitar so high it almost stuck in the ceiling, but somehow it landed in one piece, so Pete grabbed it by the neck and pounded it into the stage until it was in several dozen pieces.

Another night, the replacement equipment for The Who hadn't arrived in time for the show, so Pete asked Lek if he could borrow his amp.

"Piss off...you must be fucking joking man," was Lek's reply, but Pete promised he wouldn't destroy it and Lek reluctantly said yes. Of course, the whole tour assembled in the wings to see what fate would befall Lek's amp at the end of the show. With the customary explosions going off at the end of their final number, Pete walked to the edge of the stage in preparation to run at Lek's amp, but he misjudged his positioning, slipped, and began to fall from the twelve-foot stage. The audience probably thought what happened next was all part of the show. The five big security guards at the front of the stage saw Pete falling, caught him, and threw him back up where he landed perfectly on his feet. Immediately he began to run like a mad man at Lek's amp ('goodbye Lek's amp' we all thought), but at the last moment he jumped clean over the amplifier to thunderous applause from everybody, apart from a slightly sick-looking Lek.

The show on the 17th July in the Agrodome, Vancouver was particularly memorable, as Pete smashed his guitar up thinking he had a spare. It's remarkable to think that Pete Townshend wouldn't have a spare guitar, but there we are. Keith Moon very nearly missed the date entirely because he left his passport in his laundry in New York. It was only because it was air freighted and our charter plane detoured to pick it up in Seattle, that he was allowed to enter Canada.

As 'normal' as Roger Daltrey was off-stage, on-stage he was a dynamo…absolutely brimming with electric stage presence. After a series of microphone spinning mishaps, it became necessary for the road crew to apply an abundance of gaffer tape around his mic cable to prevent his microphone from flying into the crowd at Mach 3. Roger was also cursed with having so much nervous energy after a show that he struggled to sleep. To make the most of a night off on one occasion, we decided to make a morning flight to the next city so that we could hit the town that night without having to get up early the next morning. While we were flying, I thought I'd help Roger with his sleep problem, so I went to the galley to make some sandwiches and tea for everyone. Roger's sandwich was different to the others – I'd loaded it with crushed up sleeping tablets. We landed at the next city at 3pm where Roger went straight to bed, and didn't resurface for twenty-four hours, while the rest of us painted the town red. I didn't tell him about the naughty sandwich until the end of the tour, but he thanked me and told me it was the best sleep he'd had.

Keith Moon would have been a relatively normal guy if he could have limited himself to just two beers. But of course, he never had just two beers. He was the most incredible fun to tour with and took practical joking to a level higher than even we aspired to. The line between sanity and insanity is very fine indeed.

One night the whole tour was stopping in the same hotel. The three-storey building had three sides, in the middle of which was a swimming pool. Lek and I were with our manager, Charlie Silverman, on a second-floor balcony where Charlie had bet us $50 that we couldn't jump into the pool without breaking any bones. After a little discussion, the bet was all but sealed when we heard an almighty scream from the roof. We looked up to see Keith Moon jump off the roof wearing a cape and a top hat, before landing in the deep end (which was only six feet deep).

"Bet's off," said Charlie, tearing the $50 from my hand.

Once wasn't enough for Keith, though, and he did it another four times, and even got the flight engineer to join him, expanding their repertoire to spins and twists. It was surprising that nobody ever got seriously hurt, although the fact that everybody was well anaesthetised probably helped. The flight attendant had very sore feet the next day but Keith was all right because he had been wearing jackboots, of course.

Keith's favourite new discovery on this, his first American trip, was the cherry bomb. A cherry bomb is a small, golf ball-sized firework that emits a loud bang with quite a bit of force – it's essentially a tiny hand grenade, and very easy to conceal in a pocket. Bobby Vee and his band had introduced us to the fun-sized bomb the previous year on a run of shows. On one occasion we were following behind them on the way to a gig when about ten smoking objects came flying out of their windows and exploded directly beneath our car. The noise was deafening.

Needless to say, Keith Moon was delighted when we introduced him to the cherry bomb. One morning we were checking out of a hotel, and when Keith politely said to the receptionist that he'd forgotten something in his room, I knew he was up to some mischief, so I followed him. Back at his room, he went straight to the bathroom, pulled out a cherry bomb, lit the fuse and dropped it in the toilet. With precision timing he flushed the toilet, and the bomb exploded just as it rounded the u-bend, which shattered, sending water in every direction. With the u-bend now missing, the whole toilet fell off the wall rupturing the main water supply, which, in turn sent a water jet across the bathroom. He turned around and walked out as if nothing had happened. On the way out, he even had the nerve to tell the receptionist that he'd been ripped off for a phone call he didn't make. What Keith never considered was that Herman's Hermits footed the bills for hotel damage!

Our record for one night of juvenile destruction amounted to $25,000, which was at the Holiday Inn in Flint, Michigan, 23rd August 1967. It was Keith Moon's and my joint 21st birthday. It all started so innocently. The entire tour was gathered in the dining room where there were a few birthday cakes for Keith, a couple of cakes for my birthday (which was a few weeks before) and a few dozen other cakes for everybody else in the entourage. The cakes, along with paper plates and napkins, filled a large table in the middle of the room – it was an impressive sight. Keith Moon was about to get stuck into a cake when I stopped him, just as a fork-full was about to go into his mouth.

"What the fuck are you playing at?" he protested.

I told him that we don't know who had baked the cakes or what was in them. I explained that somebody had sent us a poisoned cake the year before, and we'd had another cake with razor blades in, so we were now very cautious. Keith put his plate back on the table and pondered for a moment. Eventually, he stuck his fingers into the top of the cake and proceeded to flick the cream into the face of Karl, who was standing next to him. Everybody in the room laughed hysterically except for Karl, who plunged his fingers into the nearest cake and returned the compliment to Keith. Within seconds, and reminiscent of an old slapstick movie, everybody in the room was hurling cake at each other, and within five minutes the room resembled the inside of a cake. There was cake on the walls, on the ceiling, trodden into the carpet.

When there was no more cake to throw, Moonie went over to Karl and ripped his trouser leg from the pocket down to the knee, then proceeded to laugh in his face. Karl was never one to shirk such a challenge, so he grabbed Keith's trousers and pulled so hard that it ripped the stitching down every seam. Now, Mr. Moon wasn't wearing any underpants, and his t-shirt was far too short to cover his privates, which everybody in the room thought extremely funny, all except for a police officer who was, up to this point, supposed to be guarding us from the outside world. When he saw Keith's undercarriage flailing around, he took out his revolver and walked over to Keith to arrest him for breaking Michigan State decency laws. The most amusing aspect was that the officer was pointing his gun at Keith's manhood, as if he was going to shoot it if it tried to run off. As we laughed at this, the officer pulled out his handcuffs and tried to restrain Keith, but we were too quick and too many for him, and managed to separate them long enough for Keith's roadie and his tour manager to frogmarch him out of the nearest exit. As he was bundled out of the door, he tripped and fell face first onto the ground, smashing out his two front teeth. He spent most of the night in an emergency dental hospital having his mouth rearranged, but he was so high it took three guys to hold him down while the dentist worked on him.

Meanwhile, back at the Holiday Inn, the police officer was slipped $100 for his good work and sent on his way after being assured that the damage would be paid for in the morning. Peter and I decided to clean the cake off each other using fire extinguishers, which seemed like a good idea at the time, but of course it turned into another boisterous fight. We were all over the hotel, in and out of rooms, and when your fire extinguisher ran out, you just grabbed another off the wall. The fight spilled out into the car park, but we eventually ran out of extinguishers, so I decided to go back to my room.

From my room I noticed an adjoining door wide open and could see a couple of roadies and some girls drinking, so I went in and joined their party. One of the roadies was called Horse (because of his size). He was chatting up one of the girls, so I went over to blow him out. I made a remark about him being three hundred pounds of dynamite with a one-inch fuse, and while he was laughing, I walked the girl into my room. A few seconds later, he presumably got the joke, and banged on the door swearing he would kill me when he got his hands on me.

"Go fuck yourself," I bravely shouted from behind the locked door. But no sooner had I finished the sentence, the door, its wooden surround, and half a dozen bricks came flying into my room. Through the dust, Horse emerged with a murderous look in his eyes. Recognising that I was about to get my arse well and truly kicked I quickly said that I was joking – that it was British humour and prompted the girl to go with him. He left my room giving me a knowing wink, and said he'd see me in the morning. I leant what was left of the door against the gap and went to bed.

The next morning the tour manager paid for the damage, which we all denied involvement in. The damage also included two hundred feet of missing railing from around the swimming pool, and most of the pool furniture that had mysteriously disappeared. A lawyer recently asked me if it was true that Keith Moon had driven a car into the swimming pool that night, to which I replied: "Nah…he was too pissed to drive."

By the time the dentist had rebuilt Keith's mouth, they'd missed the departure of our plane and had to charter another one in order to get to Philadelphia in time for the show. Apparently, the plane they hired flew through a ferocious storm and nearly crashed. Karl told me that at one point the plane dropped so fast that the dust on the floor hit the ceiling, along with everything else that wasn't strapped down.

That night saw both Herman's Hermits and The Who receive lifetime bans from ever staying in a Holiday Inn. Between you and I, they now seem to have forgotten about this.

Towards the end of the North American stretch of this tour (early September), Lek and I befriended two girls at the Ohio State Fair, and we arranged to spend a day off with them on one of their father's speedboat. On the morning, they picked us up from our hotel and drove us out to where the boat was moored. We took it in turns helming the boat, getting braver and braver with our speed on each turn. I remember sitting in the back while Lek was powering over waves, and at one point took us clean over our own wake. As he turned to gauge my reaction, his sunglasses left his head and flew into the water. Of course, I thought this was hilarious. Now it was my turn. I pushed the throttle as far as it would go, to the point that at times only the motor was in contact with the water. We were going so fast that a rattling sound started, which I presumed to be the engine. I looked around and quickly realised the sound was Lek's wig flapping up and down against his forehead. I burst into laughter as he held onto his hairpiece as he tried to ensure it didn't end up in the same place as his sunglasses.

Thirty-odd years later, one of the girls emailed me to ask if I remember the day on the speedboat in Ohio…I mailed back to say I could never forget the day I thought I'd blown the engine up, and had a quiet chuckle about Lek's flailing wig.

While we were having a blast in Ohio, The Who had flown to Los Angeles where the four-track tapes of I Can See For Miles and Rael were mixed and mastered. Rock and roll never sleeps.

Back on the road on the 8th September at the Anaheim Convention Centre, Los Angeles, and having watched the rest of the group smash up their instruments, John Entwistle set to work on his bass guitar, but the thing just wouldn't break. It took a good ten minutes to smash it up, with the auditorium now in complete silence, aside from the rest of The Who shouting their encouragement. Surreal.

My other enduring memory of The Who on that tour was their love of using stage explosives. Normally, the explosives would be used in their own set, and to great effect. But on the very last night of the tour, in Honolulu, Hawaii, they had so much explosive powder left that one of them, I suspect Keith, told their road manager to put it all beneath my drum stool as we played. At the end of the last number, I'm Henry the VIII, I Am, they threw the switch causing an enormous bang, a blinding flash and a ridiculous amount of smoke. If you've seen the film, This Is Spinal Tap, you may remember a scene with an exploding drummer – this was very similar. The explosion burnt the back of my shirt and ignited my hair, and the blast rendered my hearing temporarily useless. When the smoke cleared, they were amazed to see me standing and still smiling from ear to ear. Whilst it is an honour to be blown up by The Who, I suspect this incident is probably responsible for the hearing problem I have to this day.

A few days after this tour concluded, we appeared with The Who on US TV show, The Smothers Brothers Comedy Hour (aired on 24th September). After we'd done our bit, The Who mimed to I Can See for Miles, and a specially recut version of My Generation, which even had the sound of them smashing their instruments at the end. Unbeknown to anybody, Keith Moon had filled his bass drum with far in excess of safe levels of flash powder. When they reached the end of the song, the resulting explosion literally shook the cameras and blew out the studio monitors. Pete, who was stood nearest to the blast, temporarily lost his hearing, as Keith rolled on the floor, concussed, bleeding, and with a three-inch gash in his arm. At this apogee of commotion, Tommy Smothers emerged from the wings with an acoustic guitar around his neck, which Pete ripped from him and smashed into pieces on the studio floor. Screen legend, Bette Davis, who was awaiting her cue in the wings, apparently fainted into the arms of fellow guest, Mickey Rooney. It was just another normal day on the road with The Who.

Following North America, the next two months saw us continue to globetrot, touring Singapore, Denmark, Brazil, Argentina, Mexico and the UK. In October, we turned down the chance to play at the coronation of the Shah of Iran in his royal palace, in favour of a well-needed holiday.

In December, we began a ten-day engagement at the Statler-Hilton Hotel, Miami, Florida. I had recently married, so my first wife, Dale, joined us on this trip. It was as close to a honeymoon as we were likely to get.

During the Miami residency, we recorded an episode of the Jackie Gleason Show (which would be aired 10th February 1968). I was a big fan of Jackie Gleason in the Honeymooners show, so I was very much looking forward to meeting him. The show went well, and afterwards we were invited to go and see The Supremes (who were also guests on the show) who were performing in the hotel. The show was fantastic, but one guy sitting opposite our table had a problem with us being given the VIP treatment. As soon as the show finished, this guy got very aggressive and a fight broke out. Another man tried to intervene in order to calm things, but mister angry put paid to him by swinging an empty champagne bottle round his head. Before you knew it there was blood, women screaming, and all hell let loose. In the melee, the aggressor and his party then tried to leave without paying their bill, but Karl gave chase. He caught up with them outside and grabbed the car's door handle in an attempt to stop them driving away, which of course didn't work. The driver accelerated away dragging Karl with him. Karl, realising he had to let go, did so, and took a few rolls down the street. Luckily, he only had a few scratches.

Shortly afterwards, we were all in the Supremes' dressing room talking to Diana Ross, while my wife, who was a state registered nurse, tended to the head of the man who'd been hit with the champagne bottle.

1967 stats…

Singles (UK): There's A Kind Of Hush (Peak No.7)

Singles (US): There's A Kind Of Hush (Peak No. 4)
Don't Go Out Into The Rain (Peak No. 18)
Museum (Peak No. 39)

Albums (US): There's A Kind Of Hush All Over The World (Peak No.13)
Blaze (Peak No.75)

7

The Sixties draw to a close

By 1968, the British Invasion was beginning to fizzle out. We all still enjoyed enormous popularity, but that fervour and insanity that had greeted us in early 1965 was on the wane. Apart from The Beatles (who were continuing to reinvent pop music with every release) and The Rolling Stones, the likes of Herman's Hermits, Gerry & the Pacemakers, The Zombies, The Yardbirds, The Small Faces, The Spencer Davis Group, The Tremeloes, The Dave Clark Five, The Hollies, The Searchers, The Animals, Freddie & The Dreamers, Petula Clark and Dusty Springfield – the acts that had all but dominated the US charts for the previous four or five years – would now find it a struggle to trouble the Billboard top twenty. The invasion bands now gave way to a new breed of American artists that had been heavily influenced by the British domination. Acts like The Byrds, Gary Puckett, The Box Tops and The Turtles (along with a still vigorous Motown and a new, heavier shade of rock), were now the preferred flavour of the American record-buying audience.

But that didn't stop us being busy. Aside from January and February, which, courtesy of Peter being busy filming Pinocchio for Disney in the States, and giving the rest of us an extended break, the calendar was still full of tours, one-off shows, and TV appearances. Over the next twelve months we would embark on an Argentinian tour, a tour of Germany and Italy (with John Paul Jones on keyboards), a UK spring tour (with Amen Corner, Dave Berry, John Rowles, The Echoes, Johnny Ball, and The Paper Dolls), a three-week European tour (with Procol Harum and Dave Dee, Dozy, Beaky, Mick & Tich), visits to Israel, Philippines and Australia, a ten-day engagement in Canada, two US tours, and another two-week stint in Germany playing US Air Force bases. As if that wasn't enough, we also squeezed in umpteen TV shows, and Peter managed to find time to get married on his twenty-first birthday (5th November). We were supposed to tour France in May of 1968, but it coincided with a revolt, general strike and huge political upheaval, so the tour was cancelled.

On 12th September, the movie, Mrs. Brown, You've Got A lovely Daughter was released. The film's critical reception wasn't brilliant, but the songs ensured a positive legacy.

It was after one such TV recording (the Basil Brush Show in July) that we were travelling from north London back home to Manchester, when we had one of our many transport related mishaps. Our roadie at the time, Jeff Hanlon, started the engine, slipped into first gear, then released the clutch, but to our collective surprise absolutely nothing happened. Jeff opened the bonnet and we peered inside for a while pretending we knew what we were looking for. We eventually deduced that the van's accelerator cable had broken. We weren't members of either of the roadside recovery services available, and, being about seven o'clock in the evening, there was nowhere open to get it fixed. But Jeff came up with a solution.

He needed a bass string off Karl's guitar, which could be attached to the carburettor, fed through the passenger window, where Karl could pull it to open up the carburettor and give us forward motion. It was a master plan. We got back in the van and Jeff started the engine, before giving Karl instruction:

"When I say 'pull', pull the string to give us revs, and when I say 'off', relax the tension on the guitar string."

Within a few minutes they had developed a steady system, and as we headed towards the M1 motorway, the rest of us had all but forgotten that the double-act in the front were controlling the van's revolutions with a 0.046 inch, flatwound guitar string. When we got on the motorway, Jeff instructed Karl to adjust the tension until we could maintain a steady eighty miles per hour, which he duly did. However, after a long day in the TV studio, Karl was naturally very tired and, without telling Jeff, decided to tie the string around the window handle and take a little nap. This wasn't a problem until Jeff noticed that we were running low on fuel, and made the decision to pull into the next services, which was just half a mile ahead of us.

"Release the string," Jeff requested, but Karl was in deep sleep. "Let the string go," he now shouted, as we hurtled towards the slip road at eighty miles per hour, but Karl utterly refused to stir.

Jeff was fully aware that we didn't have enough fuel to get to the next services, so it was vital that we made this stop. Now we all shouted at Karl and he eventually woke up as we were half way up the slip road.

"What's going on?" he replied in his disorientation.

"Untie the fucking bass string!" somebody shouted.

"We're all going to die!" somebody else shouted (I think it was me).

We are now beyond the point where we can rejoin the motorway, and all I can see is Karl clumsily trying to untie the string as the petrol station gets closer and closer. With moments to spare, Karl released the string, and Jeff brought us to a stop in a cloud of smoke and screeching tyres, directly beside a petrol pump. Jeff was far too cool, and climbed out of the van through the rubbery smog, and filled the van up as if nothing had happened. The rest of us were in a state of abject shock, and after a much-needed visit to the toilet we resumed our trip home making sure that Karl remained awake for the rest of the journey.

It was fair to say that the cracks were beginning to show in 1968. As well as him filming Pinocchio, Peter was in demand for more and more projects, and in July he managed to stay on holiday in Ibiza for too long, and some dates and a TV recording in Scotland had to be cancelled. Lek and Karl also kept themselves busy on a variety of recording sessions for other artists. It was the first time since 1964 that we weren't with each other for twenty-four hours a day. We were still very busy, but gaps were opening up. In spite of this, we still kept putting records out and enjoyed something of a resurgence in the UK hit parade, having only had one hit in 1967.

In April 1969, we pulled out of a tour (with The Love Affair) after three nights because of half-full houses; the promoter had not done his job. This controversy led to speculation in the press that it spelled the end for the package tours that had been so hugely successful until then, but here we are – over fifty years later – and they're as popular as ever. But it was a fair assumption at the time, after all, music was changing, and the way live acts were booked was changing. We were still playing many tours (packaged or otherwise), but cropping up more and more in our diaries were one- or two-week long cabaret engagements, a brand of show which would become more and more popular over the next two decades.

But back on the road…from the summer of 1969, we were off globetrotting again. Israel, Hong Kong, Philippines, Australia, the US and Mexico were all on the itinerary, followed by a tour of Canada and some European dates, then back to the Talk of the Town in London for a critically very well-received two-week engagement.

At the end of 1969, we were once again entrusted to appear in a pantomime, this time at the Odeon Theatre in Streatham, London. The show was Aladdin, who was played by Peter, whilst the rest of us played Chinese policemen!

It seems to be a showbiz truth that you get offered Pantomime either when you're on your way up, or on your way down.

At first, the Hermits weren't keen on the production as we were barely in it until the last twenty minutes, so after a meeting with our agent and the producers, it was agreed that our money would be upped, and bigger parts were written into the script for us. With the proposition now more palatable, I rented a beautiful flat in Maida Vale where my wife, Dale, and our daughter, Emma, could stay with me for the duration of the pantomime. The place had a fabulous lounge with a concert grand piano – it was no good to me, but it certainly looked the part.

With Norman Vaughan cast as the funny man, a good wage negotiated, and the chance to spend some time with my family, Aladdin was shaping up to be an enjoyable run. With our circumstances very different to the end of 1964, it would be hard to get up to the level of mischief that we reached during Dick Whittington, but it was still effortless for Peter to upset one of the stagehands to the point of vindictive retribution. The stagehand got his own back by fixing Noone's magic carpet so that it got jammed twenty-five feet above the stage. Peter was up there for twenty minutes as his carpet swung in and out of view above the stage, and it took the whole intermission to fix the problem and get him down. Then, a few nights later somebody slashed all four of Peter's tyres on his car. I'm sure he thought it was one of us, but it wasn't, it was merely one of the side effects of treating people badly.

Back in the theatre, I and another actor had to carry the princess on stage in a sedan chair, in the scene where she is supposed to marry Aladdin (which had to be rewritten because

Peter refused to kiss the Princess). Each night or so, unawares to me, the other lads in the band added a stage weight to the chair, so by the end of the run it was virtually impossible to lift, and on the last night we had to drag the chair with the princess sat in it, across the stage. Even when the princess had got out, it was still to heavy to shift, so it was painstakingly dragged into the wings. I think the audience thought it was part of the show. On the last night the lads lifted the skirt around the chair to show me what they'd done. I counted eighteen stage weights – which was about four hundred and fifty pounds, which, added to the chair and the weight of the princess meant we were attempting to lug a six-hundred-pound box!

After a few weeks in London, I got a phone call from my Dad who told me that somebody had broken into my house in Manchester and stolen all my gold records as well as the TV set and a variety of other personal things. Back then we had a cleaner that came twice a week and it was she that made the discovery. Two days later, some people moved into the ground floor flat next door to us in Maida Vale and opened up a bakery. The smell of the fresh bread in the mornings was lovely, but within days I started to notice mouse dropping in our kitchen, followed, a couple of days later, by the sight of a mouse rolling a walnut cross the floor under the grand piano. The next day I saw one climbing up inside the curtain, so I got the poker from the fire place and beat the curtain from top to bottom. It was time for Mouse Hunt!

Dale warned me that if I didn't get rid of them, she was taking Emma back to Manchester. So, the next day before going to the Odeon, I went to a hardware shop and bought six mousetraps. When I got back that night, I went about setting all the traps – three in the kitchen and three in the lounge. My mistake was not telling Dale that I'd set the traps. The next morning before I woke, Dale had taken Emma out of her cot so she could crawl around. She crawled around all right, straight into the kitchen where I had set three of the traps. I was awakened by a very loud scream. I rushed into the kitchen to find a hysterical Emma with a mousetrap, one on each hand. As I was trying to remove the traps, I saw a mouse run under refrigerator just as Dale came into the kitchen. There was another loud scream, this time from Dale, which started Emma crying again. I pulled the refrigerator out to find the mouse running down the back of it, so I grabbed a big wooden spoon and tried to hit the mouse as it ran round the cooling pipes. I missed it and it jumped to the floor and ran between Dales legs and into the lounge. That very same day, Dale and Emma were on the train back to Manchester.

1968 stats ...

Singles (UK):   I Can Take Or Leave Your Loving (Peak No.11)
Sleepy Joe (Peak No.12)
Sunshine Girl (Peak No.8)
Something's Happening (Peak No.6)

Singles (US):   I Can Take Or Leave Your Loving (Peak No.22)

                Sleepy Joe (Peak No.61)
                Sunshine Girl (Peak No.101)
                The Most Beautiful Thing In My Life
                (Peak No.131)
                Something's Happening (Peak No.130)

Albums (US):   Mrs Brown, You've Got A Lovely Daughter
                (Peak No.182)

1969 stats ...

Singles (UK):   My Sentimental Friend (Peak No.2)
                Here Comes The Star (Peak No.33)

8

The Not-so Swinging Seventies

By early 1970, owing to the number of projects Peter (particularly) was involved in, press speculation over a split became heightened. In one interview (New Musical Express), Peter was somewhat callous in his response to the allegation; "There's no question of splitting up, the Hermits could do two one-nighters a week to earn some money, because when I'm working on my own, they're more or less on the dole."

Peter, our management and our record company, may have been insistent that there was no split on the horizon, but life within the band was becoming more fractious. We had to turn down a summer tour of Australia because Peter couldn't face spending thirty hours on an aeroplane. Then, for our fourteen-week summer season engagement at Great Yarmouth, we ended up being billed as Peter Noone & Herman's Hermits, and pretty much every subsequent show after had the same billing. The final insult came when our last single release, Lady Barbara, came out with the same credit.

But Peter couldn't go anywhere just yet, as we contractually owed MGM (our American label) a lot of tracks.

Between 1968 and 1970, we recorded fifty songs for MGM Records, but as acid rock and progressive rock became more popular, as well as the surge of The Monkees (who were very much in our segment of the market), the record company through all their promotional might behind new acts, leaving Herman's Hermits' American chart ambitions very much in limbo. As a result, four new albums of material and a compilation album were shelved, and never to be released. All of those recordings sadly remain unissued, aside from a song called Searching For The Southern Sun, which ended up on the B-side of Bet Yer Life I Do.

In spite of all of this, the constantly spinning roundabout of gigs and TV appearances continued. Package tours were giving way to weeklong cabaret engagements, but we still completed short tours of Ireland and West Africa, played the Royal Variety Performance, and did a two-week stint at the London Palladium.

In December I rented out my 1957 S-type Bentley so Jimmy Ruffin could be driven around London in style for five weeks.

Again, in spite of insistences from our management, throughout 1971 and into early 1972, circumstances saw the band and Peter slowly drift apart. Peter released his first solo single (David Bowie's Oh You Pretty Things) and when it became clear that Peter was too busy to fulfil our ever-busy schedule, we recruited Manchester guitarist/songwriter Peter Cowap to replace him in our live shows and TV appearances.

Billed now as The Hermits, we released our debut single (with Peter Cowap on lead vocals) She's A Lady, which was written by Geoff Foot, who would join us many years later, in 1989. Released on the RCA Victor label, the single was co-produced by Eric Stewart, forging another connection between the Hermits and 10cc. As well as the single, we recorded an album, A Whale Of A Tale, but like our MGM recordings, the album release was shelved by RCA. It was a tough time to be a Hermit, and because of these frustrations, at the end of 1972, Keith Hopwood left the band to concentrate on building Pluto Recording Studios in Manchester, and Peter Cowap also defected to pursue other interests. Now, with only three original members remaining, resilience determination would be required for the Hermits to survive.

So, heading into 1973, we recruited nineteen-year-old rising star, John Gaughan (from Leeds) to complete a new four-piece line-up of the Hermits.

1970 stats ...

Singles (UK): Years May Come, Years May Go (Peak No.7)
Bet Yer Life I Do (Peak No.22)
Lady Barbara (Peak No.13)
(Credited as: Peter Noone & Herman's Hermits)

1971 stats ...

Albums (UK): The Most Of Herman's Hermits (Peak No.14)

Life went on.

By the middle of 1973, even though it was less than ten years since us, and a number of other UK acts, were at the very height of conquering America, we were officially confirmed to the 'nostalgia' pigeonhole. Richard Nader, a promoter who specialised in compiling package tours of 'oldies acts' came up with the British Invasion Tour of 1973, and quickly secured the services of us, The Searchers, Wayne Fontana & the Mindbenders, Gerry & the Pacemakers, and Billy J Kramer & the Dakotas. Even though Peter had left the band two years before, he'd negotiated a fee for this tour, meaning we were almost the original line-up, aside from Keith, who had left in 1972.

On the first day of the Invasion tour, Peter pulled up in front of the bus in his Mercedes. He'd arranged that he and his wife would travel separately to the rest of the tour, which had already become a source of agitation. But when it was time to start up and drive to the first venue, his car refused to start and he was forced to board the bus to a very loud, ironic cheer.

Considering how radically musical tastes had changed in the previous ten years, the tour was a huge hit. Many commentators were surprised to see this bygone line-up pulling 13,000 people through the doors of Madison Square Garden, and reviews of our set were equally positive – perhaps they thought we might have forgotten how to play since they last saw us.

Halfway through the tour, Ray Reneri made the mistake of telling me that Noone had managed to up his money to $60,000, which was about eight times the originally agreed sum. This is the reason why, when he asked to rejoin the band in 1975, we wanted equal shares, but he insisted on 60% for him and 40% for the rest of us. Naturally, we told him to go fuck himself.

Music Industry Insight #214

Following the British Invasion tour of 1973, our tour manager, Ray Reneri, became the band's manager proper (for US business), and would remain so for eight years. It took us a long time to realize that he was ripping us off, and we wouldn't have found out at all if it weren't for the fact that kept seeing different brandings of our albums in truck stops across the USA. Of course, when we became aware of them, we asked Ray to investigate, although it would be a hard thing to track down. Some years later he confessed that he'd borrowed $10,000 from some less-than-pleasant people in New York City, and when it came to paying them back, he had no money, and was to be on the receiving end of some nasty retribution. So, to settle his debt, he gave them the master tapes of our new recordings, which they pressed and distributed as reimbursement. Shortly after this admission we had a band meeting, and Ray was no longer our manager.

Hialeah Park Race Track, Miami, 1974. I went to the horse races with the rest of the group while playing a two-week engagement at the Seven Seas Lounge, Newport Hotel. It was a beautiful day...not a cloud in the sky and about eighty in the shade. We got there around noon and had a good look around to check the place out. We found the bar, the paddock and a pizza place, what more could you ask for aside from a couple of winners? I got myself a program and studied the form of each horse (like I knew what I was doing) then went to the paddock to see the horse I fancied, before placing a bet on it and heading back to the bar for a beer. When each race came under starter's orders, I would go into the stands to watch my horse run, which is putting it rather optimistically; I was having some bad luck.

This routine went on for the next ten races; paddock, beer, pizza, stand, lose money. With one race left and ten beers inside me, I decided it was time for a change in strategy. This time I went for a beer first then visited the paddock to weigh up the talent.

They led the horses out for all to see. The last horse out caught my attention, what with his sad eyes and bowed back. He looked like he'd been pulling a milk float all day without a rest. I checked the horse out in the program to see its form – it didn't have any, and neither did his Puerto Rican jockey. When I saw that his odds were thirty-to-one, I knew that this was the horse for me. For the last nine races I had bet on the horse with the best form, and I wasn't going to play their game anymore!

I checked my pockets to see how much money I had left – a grand total of $13 – and went straight to the stand to put my bet on, then went for my last beer. When the race started, I wasn't surprised to see that my horse was flailing in last place and that the favorite was in the lead. By half way, though, my horse was starting to gain on the leaders, and when it rounded the last bend, my horse took off and managed to get ten lengths ahead of the pack. I was the only person in the place cheering as it romped past the post.

"You didn't have a bet on that horse, did you?" asked a confused Karl.

"I bloody well did," I replied, still in disbelief.

That was my first and last experience at the horses. When we got back to the Newport Hotel it was straight down to the bar, and you guessed it, it was my round until all my $335 of winnings had disappeared. Never mind…it was a great day out.

After another show at the Seven Seas Lounge, we were all invited to a party on our day off by one of the barmen who worked at the venue. The party was in a house, which, typical of many properties in Florida, backed onto an expansive waterway…the water's edge and the garden met. The weather was glorious, and courtesy of a plentiful supply of cold beer and barbecued food, we were soon in a hearty party spirit. During the evening I was told by our barman of a good old American party trick to welcome girls as they entered the party. Basically, when a girl arrives, you tell them they can only stay if they can pass a simple initiation test. The test is as follows: a newspaper rolled into a conical shape is put down the front of their T-Shirt or dress. They then have to lean their head back and balance a half dollar coin on their foreheads before they are instructed to roll their head forward and catch the coin in the newspaper. Simple…if they could catch the coin in the cone, they could stay at the party. Of course, what we didn't tell them was when they leaned their head back with a half dollar coin on their forehead, we would pour a pitcher of ice-cold water into the cone. We did this a couple of times and the girls received it humorously, before we gave them a Herman's Hermits tour T-Shirt to change into.

It was almost dark when the front door bell rang, and as I was nearest to the door, I answered it. To my surprise there was a beautiful looking girl standing there in a full-length evening dress, so I invited her in and explained the rules of initiation. She said it sounded silly but fun, and was all for it. When the ice-cold water went down the front of her evening dress, she let out a deafening scream. We all started to laugh as her head came back so fast that the coin flew out of the window. She looked at me with pure hate in her eyes, kneed me in the balls then punched me in the mouth. I was sent across the room backwards, smashed into a wall and slid down it with stars circling my head. The lads calmed her down and gave her a tour T-Shirt, while I went outside onto the balcony and attempted to nurse my balls back to life and stop the bleeding from my lip. After a few minutes of rubbing, I began to feel a bit better.

As I glanced out over the water, still cupping myself, I could just make out what appeared to be a man sitting in the middle of the lake on a small island about a hundred and fifty yards from the shore. I went down to the water's edge for a better look and realized it was Dave Barrow, our bass player. I called out his name but got no reply. I started to get worried as it was nearly dark, and the waters of Florida are full of things that want to kill you at the best of times. Being a few beers over the common-sense limit, I dived in and swam out to him. He was frozen with fear. I asked him if he was hurt, but he merely replied that he couldn't swim back alone, so I said we would swim back together nice and slowly.

We started to swim back gently, but then became aware of a pair of eyes sticking out of the water. Then another pair of eyes appeared to our left. I told Dave that perhaps we should swim a little faster. Then I heard a splash behind us. I turned around in the water to see two more pairs of eyes had joined us.

"Now would be a fucking good time to pretend you're an Olympic swimmer, Dave," I said as calmly as I could.

"Why?" he replied.

"Because if we don't get back to the shore pretty darned quickly, Herman's Hermits will become a duo."

Encouraged by the shouts of "faster you bastards" coming from the shore, we swam faster than we knew we could. We made it back just in time to see the eyes disappear back into the water. After a couple of shots of Jack Deniels, we were ready to party again. The girl in the evening dress now looked at me as some kind of a hero, and spent the rest of the night all over me.

17th February, 1975. Ray Reneri had set up a guest appearance at a three-day showcase being held at a large hotel in Des Moines, Iowa. A showcase is an industry event where lots of entertainers entertain, and lots of agent's book. It's basically a musical cattle market. We arrived on the second day as we were closing the show on the third and final night, so it was a party night for us.

The evening meal was an enormous buffet, at the centre of which was the biggest pig I've ever seen, complete with a large apple in its mouth. After attacking the buffet and imbibing numerous beers, I decided the time was right to go to bed, but as was often the case, I was persuaded by the boys to have just one more. An hour later, I again tried to go to bed, but the lads said they didn't believe I was going to bed alone so insisted on following me to my room to see for themselves.

I entered my room, which was dark except for the light over the bed. Clearly illuminated beneath the light was a lump under my bed covers, so naturally I went over to investigate. Pulling back the sheets I was shocked to see the pig's head lying in my bed, staring back at me. Of course, the lads all thought it was hilarious.

By the time I'd got the pig's head out of my bed, and attempted to clean up the mess it had left, I was wide awake, so decided to head back to the bar for a couple more drinks. But I didn't go alone – Mr Piggy would come for a drink as well. I concealed him in a pillowcase and went back downstairs.

In the elevator, an agent told me that Lek had got involved in a big poker game with some influential agents that book state fairs. I found the room they were playing in, showed my pass and quietly walked in. It was a serious game all right – there were hundreds of dollars in the pot, and it looked like everybody was waiting for Lek to decide whether to carry on or fold. I stood behind Lek's chair while everybody looked at him...the tension was palpable.

After a while I could contain myself no more. I reached into the pillowcase, pulled out the pig's head, and threw it into the centre off the table. Everybody recoiled in horror as the head rolled across the pile of money.

"Lek raises the pot by a pig's head," I shouted in jest, but the people around the table were not amused, so I made a hasty exit.

But the story of my antics spread throughout the hotel very quickly, and before long I was having drinks bought for me by complete strangers, all eager to hear the story. It turned into a very late night.

During yet another tour of the USA in 1975, Karl had such a bad throat that he didn't think he could make it through a full show. It was suggested that he bought some honey, then, each time his throat gave him discomfort, he could take a swig. We were in Wisconsin at the time and, unlike in the UK where it was still sold in glass jars, in the States honey was sold in squeezable plastic bottles. And so, every couple of songs throughout the show he would go back to his amplifier and help himself to a throat full of the soothing nectar. About half way through the gig he went back for his fix, but this time squeezed too hard, firing the plastic top off the bottle, and sending honey all over his face. To make matters worse, Karl had a beard at the time, and the honey worked its way through his facial hair, and down onto his guitar. It was the funniest thing I'd seen for some time. Of course, we fell about laughing as Karl got more frustrated trying to get honey off his face and hands. It took about five minutes to regain some kind of order on stage.

March 1976

The Newport Resort Hotel on North Miami Beach had become a regular gig for us. We played in the basement of the hotel where there was a fantastic club called the Seven Seas Lounge, and we used to play it two or three times a year for two weeks at a time. As well as having a fantastic beach, there was a launch where people could put their boats in the water. On the second day of this particular stay, I was on the beach sun-bathing watching two girls struggle to pull their catamaran out of the water, so having nothing better to do, and being the sociable spirit that I am, I went over to help them. During the next few minutes of chat, I discovered they went sailing twice a week, so I said I could look after the boat and take the sails to my room for safe keeping, and if they phoned me before they were going sailing, I would get the boat ready for them as long as I could use the boat when they weren't using it. It was a good deal that suited us all.

One morning, after a heavy night drinking at the bar, I suggested that all four Hermits go for a sail on the catamaran to get some fresh air. Sailing is the perfect pick-me-up after a night on the tiles. And having owned my own seventeen-foot clinker sailing boat for several years in England, I classed myself as a fairly able sailor. We all agreed it was a good idea so we set to sea, and once we'd negotiated the breakers without any problems it was literally plain sailing.

I was at the tiller and set a course due east, and with a fair wind blowing from the north, the conditions were just about perfect as we made a steady ten knots. Within a few minutes we had all fallen asleep, myself holding the tiller. I was awoken by a large wave from a passing ship, which made our boat rock violently. In my confusion I wondered what a seafaring ship was doing so close to the shore, until I realized that it was actually us that were far out at sea. I looked at my watch; it was two hours since we had set sail. I stood up and looked around but couldn't see land. One of the lads gave me a leg up where I was just able to see what looked like a hut on the horizon.

"I can see land," I shouted down, "I think."

We headed for the little hut on the horizon until, after about twenty minutes, we realized there was something under the hut; it was a twenty-five-story hotel. What we thought was a hut was in fact the hotel elevator machinery box on top of the hotel roof. Two hours later when we finally hit the shore, we went to the pool bar for a cold beer, as we were all dehydrated.

A couple of days later Karl and I went out again on the sixteen-foot-long catamaran. With a good wind blowing we had her really going over on one keel and were once again heading out to sea when we noticed four fins breaking the water's surface about a hundred yards away. We headed to where we'd seen the fins, but there was nothing there. A moment later there was a huge bang, the boat shook violently, and I lost control of the boat to the extent that I had to let the sail down so that we could come to a stop. I pulled the rudder bar up to inspect for damage and noticed that one of the rudders had a section missing. When we got back to the beach, we dragged the boat out and took a closer look at the damaged rudder. If you ask me, I would have said that the marks on the rudder had been made with teeth, and that it had been bitten off.

Once when dining in the Ponderosa Restaurant in 1976, Karl removed a corn on the cob from his mouth to reveal his front tooth cap sticking out of the cob. We laughed of course, partially because Karl insisted that the evening's show would have to be postponed until he'd seen a dentist. When we got back to the hotel, I suggested that I might be able to stick it back in with some super glue that I had. I put him in a chair then dried the stump and cap with my hairdryer. When it was dry, I put some super glue in the cap and placed in the correct position, then told him to push down with his finger on the cap for a few seconds while it dried. After a while I told him to release the pressure, when he did, but his finger was firmly stuck to the cap, which in turn was stuck in on the stump. This caused an even greater round of laughter as Karl desperately tried to remove his finger from his tooth. He said that he definitely couldn't play with a finger stuck to his tooth, which provoked more laughter. After ten minutes of pulling and twisting, we finally managed to free his finger from the tooth, but it left a slither of skin from the top of his finger on the cap. He reluctantly did the show with some pain from his incomplete finger.

The problem with sharing a room with Lek was that he didn't like the air conditioning on in the room, whereas I liked to get the hotel room down to freezing, or as near as damn it. Pulling the bed clothes right up to neck to keep warm reminded me of when I was growing up, and we had no heating in the bedrooms. It was so cold that in the winter ice would form on the inside of our windows. But Lek liked a nice warm room and he liked to read books in bed, which meant that I would invariably fall asleep first. As soon as I fell asleep, he would get out of bed and turn the air conditioning off and carry on with his book. Then I would wake up sweating and his light would still be on as he always fell asleep reading his book, so the aircon would go back on and I'd turn his light off.

This went on for years in the USA on summer tours…the one place and time you really need air conditioning. On one occasion I woke up cooking in my own juices, so I turned the AC back on and went to the toilet. Returning, I got back into the wrong bed and fell asleep on top of him. Hours later when he awoke and could barely breathe, he thought he was paralyzed.

"What the fuck are you doing in my bed?" he shouted.

"What you doing underneath me in my bed?" I replied.

And so, it went. He was angry, but not quite as angry as the time I pissed in his suitcase.

We were sharing a room in Belgium that was so small you had to vault over your case to get into bed, and the toilet seemed to have been designed with a small child in mind. We got back from our show to find that the bar had shut, so plan B was triggered, and out came our collection of duty free. The salient facts that followed were that I got drunk and fell asleep. At some point in the middle of the night I had a vague recollection of going to what I thought was the toilet. The next morning, we all woke up late and had to dress in a hurry… there wasn't even time to put on clean clothes from our cases.

It wasn't until the next morning, whilst I was having breakfast in a different hotel, that Lek announced that he thought the van must have been letting in water because everything in his suitcase was wet. A few hours later he came up to me and called me a dirty bastard.

"What are you talking about?" I sincerely asked.

He explained that the clothes in his suitcase stunk of piss. Right then I had a flashback to the hotel room the night before, and quickly realized why I couldn't find the handle to flush the toilet.

May 1978.

Burger King had a new publicity drive called 'Have it your way or we'll pay for it'. We had been touring Florida and some other southern States playing at a chain of venues called Big Daddy's. By the time we had finished and packed the gear away it was always around three in the morning and the only places open were Danny's or Burger King. After a short drive we found a Burger King and, marching up to the counter we noticed the poster for their new promo, at which Lek starts to concoct a plan to get a free meal. Ten minutes later he orders a Whopper, and says he would like it with pickle but no sesame seeds on the bun. The poor guy behind the counter tried to explain to Lek that all the buns have sesame seeds on them, but Lek was adamant that he didn't want them and Burger King would have to pay for his meal. As was often the case with Lek, an argument broke, the police were called, and we were all thrown out of the restaurant. No supper for us that night.

A couple of nights later after performing a show at Big Daddy's, we went into a Danny's Diner for supper. We ordered with no problems and were drinking coffee when Lek decided to go to the toilet, and feeling the need too, I followed him in. The bathroom was two rows of cubicles with their backs to each other. I finished first, and as I left the rest room, I noticed a hat stand just outside the door. As quick as a flash I picked it up and took it back into the rest room. Lek was still in a cubical so I wedged the hat stand beneath the door handle so he could not get out, and childishly ran back to the table to tell the rest of boys what I'd done.

After five minutes our food arrived, but there was no sign of Lek. Just as I picked up my knife and fork the rest room door burst open and there was Lek, brandishing the hat and a ferocious look on his face.

"Very fucking funny," he shouted out at the top of his voice, and threw the hat stand at me as if it were a javelin. I saw it coming straight for me, so ducked out of the way, and it smashed into the wall behind me. The place was fairly full, and the incident sent a wave of frenzied excitement amongst the other customers. Needless to say, the manager called the police and told us to get out of his restaurant. As we were walking down the path in front of the restaurant window, we all dropped our pants and mooned the place, and to our surprise got a standing ovation from the customers. But it was another night going to bed with no supper.

Snapshots of a Life Well Lived

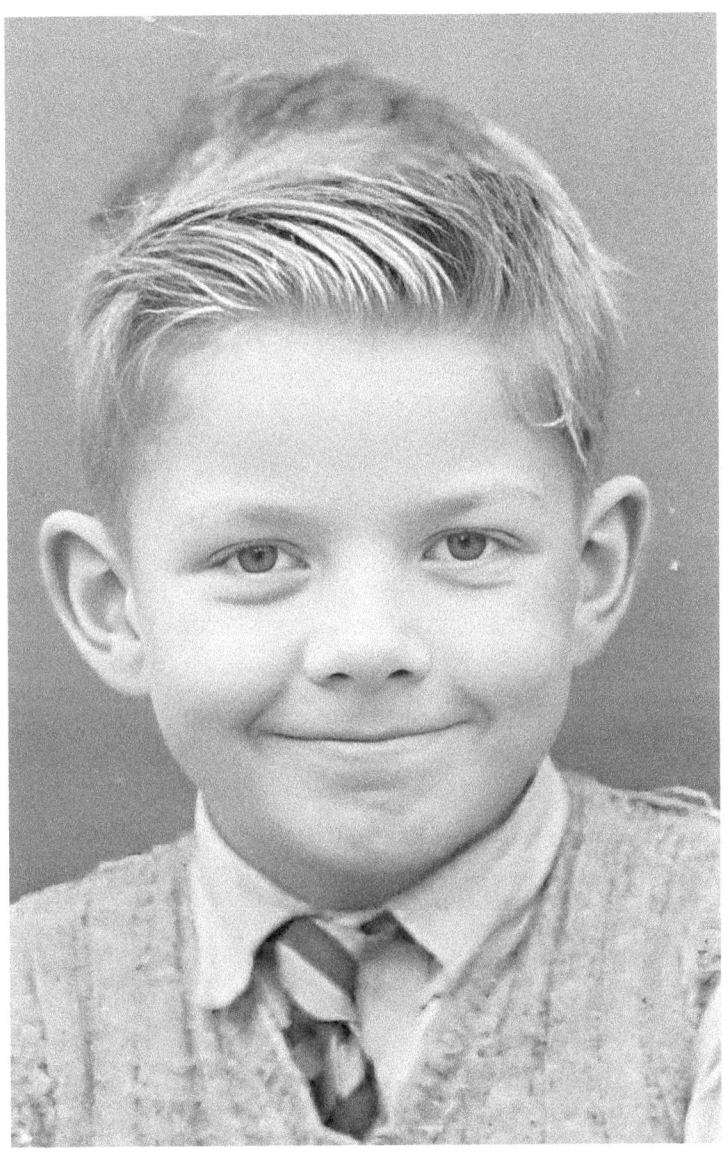

Me as a child. (Private)

Ladybarn Cup team 1960. I'm on the back row. Can you recognise me? (Private)

The Wailers. Ian Waller, Malcolm Roberts, Barry and Lek Leckenby 1962/63. (Private)

The original group 1964. Derek Lek Leckenby, Barry Whitwam, Karl Green, Keith Hopwood and Peter Noone. (Private)

My Mum & Dad. Elsie and George on a trip to California, USA when we were filming the film Hold On. (Private)

That's the way to travel to shows in the USA. (Private)

Our second plane, used for the 1966 tour with The Animals in the USA.

Our third plane, used for the 1967 tour with The Who in the USA.

Ad for 1967 tour.

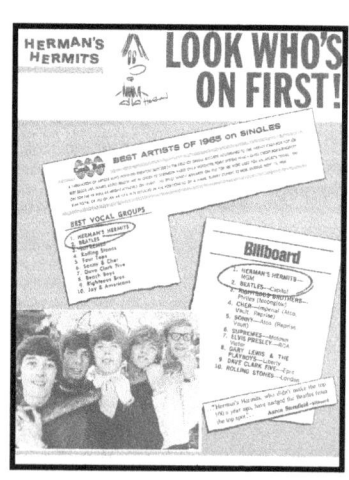

1965 promo flyer.

Recording at Kingsway Studios, London, 1965.

Together with the man responsible for me getting into a band in the first place, Mr. Elvis Presley. (Private)

Harvey Lisberg, Peter Noone, Elvis Presley, Tom Parker and I on the film set of Paradise Hawaiian Style in Hawaii in 1965. What a great day that was. (Private)

1965 publicity photo (Photo courtesy of MGM)

Promo photo for the Hold On! movie on MGM, showing Barry as an angel with wings doing a spacewalk. (PR photo)

Scene from Mrs, Brown movie 1968. (MGM PR photo)

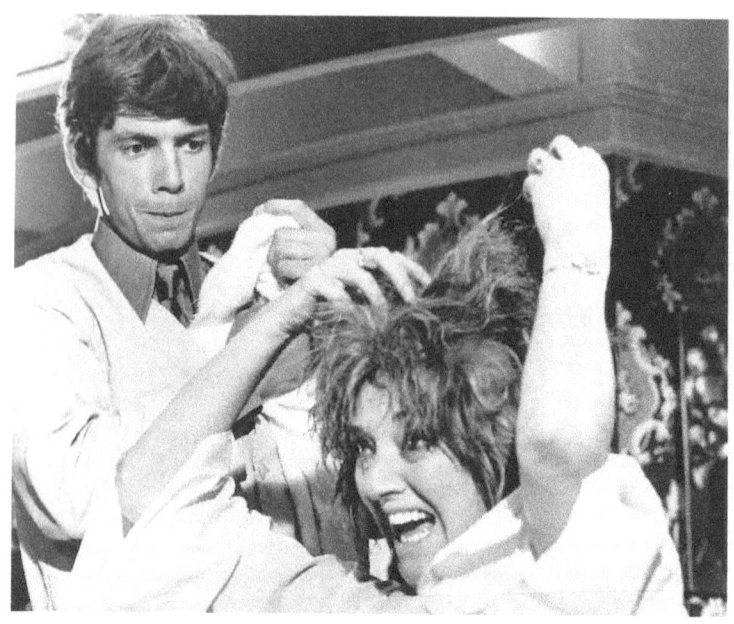

Hairdresser in the film "Mrs. Brown You're Got A Lovely Daughter". (Photo courtesy of MGM)

Having a drink in Las Vegas with Keith Moon, July 1967. (Private)

Hermits 1971, l to r: Karl Green, Peter Cowap, Keith Hopwood, Barry Whitwam and Lek Leckenby (RCA PR photo)

1974 line-up, l to r: Chris Finley, Barry Whitwam, Karl Green and Lek Leckenby (Banner Talent PR photo)

1982 line-up, l to r: Barry Whitwam, Lek Leckenby, Garth Elliott and Paul Farnell (AWP PR photo)

Together with Pat. (Private)

1989 line-up, l to r: Geoff Foot, Lek Leckenby, Rod Gerrard and Barry Whitwam (AWP PR photo)

Richard Whitwam and Proud Father at his graduation. (Private)

Peter Sarstedt and I in Germany in the 90's. (Private)

Jan Barry Whitwam with his initials JBW on the number plate of his stylish car, Burnage, 1996 (Photo: Olaf Owre)

2000 line-up, l to r: Graham Lee, Barry Whitwam, Alec Johnson and Geoff Foot (Whitwam PR photo)

Barry Whitwam in action — open air concert, Kodal, Norway, 1988 (Photo: Olaf Owre)

Barry Whitwam at Studio 26, Oslo, Norway, 1982 (Photo: Olaf Owre)

The Drifters with Barry Whitwam on a tour in USA (Private)

We toured Australia with Mike d'Abo on a big '60s revival show. Paul Jones, the other singer in Manfred Mann, was there as well. (Private)

Barry Whitwam with John Wright (left) and Harvey Lisberg, both from the band's former management, Kennedy Street Artists — open air concert, Urmston, 2013. (Photo: Olaf Owre)

This is the current lineup, l to r: Tony Young, keyboards, guitar and vocals. John Summerton, lead vocals and guitar. Jan Barry Whitwam, drums and vocals. Jamie Thurston, lead vocals and bass guitar. (Photo: Stig Ulrichsen)

2025 setup (Private)

Herman's Hermits with Don Powell from Slade in 2023.
(Photo: Stig Ulrichsen)

Here's Emma Whitwam's graduating photo. (Private)

Jono my Son-in-Law with Claire and Jove and Del the dog. (Private)

Me and Olaf Owre, Stockport, 1999. (Private)

9

The 1980s - Rock & Rollers stuck in a world of New Romantics

June 1980. It was the first night of another Ray Reneri organised US tour, and we were playing at Clinch Valley College, Wise, nestled at the south of the Blue Ridge mountains of Virginia. After the show, we were invited to a house party by one of the groups that had supported us. On the way back he explained that his house was far from finished, and that, strangely, instead of digging a basement out, he'd built it at ground floor level, and when completed he would pile tonnes of earth around it to bury the basement, thus raising the level of the ground. So, for now, one had to enter the house at basement level (which had a temporary door) because the real front door was some twenty feet up in the air. The guy who owned the house had taken the precaution of nailing this door shut so that nobody could absent-mindedly wander out to a Wile E. Coyote style demise.

When we arrived, there were already a number of people in the bottom room gathered around a beer keg on a stand, so it seemed only right to join them for a while. After a few jars, Lek emerged at the basement door covered in mud, holding a glass of Jack Daniels.

"How the hell did you get outside?" I asked, "the last time I saw you, you were upstairs."

"Well, I smoked a joint and wanted some fresh air, so I opened the door, and the next thing I knew I was down here."

Thankfully, he wasn't hurt...he just smiled and went back upstairs for another Jack. The story quickly circulated about a Hermit falling out of the lounge, which particularly surprised the owner because he said he'd used ten six-inch nails to secure the door to prevent exactly this kind of accident.

Sometime later I realised I was the only Hermit left at the party, so I asked the driver to take me back to our hotel. As we'd arrived at the party in complete darkness, I had no idea that the house was built on a small mountain amidst very undulating terrain. As I got alongside the transport, I decided to take a leak. I took two steps forward, began peeing, took another step to balance myself then – in some kind of subconscious sympathy for Lek – stepped into thin air and fell down a ravine.

The van driver had parked up right next to a substantial drop. On my way down I recall seeing the moon three times before falling through some bushes and coming to a thudding stop. I woke to a crowd looking down at me with torches, mostly amazed that I was alive. I was in no immediate pain, but then, I was heavily anaesthetised. Once I'd made myself decent (I was in mid-piss) they helped me out and made sure I was okay. I could feel a good-sized lump on my head and my head was spinning a little, but I felt I was in good enough shape to continue the journey back to the hotel.

The driver dropped me off before gunning off in a cloud of rubber smoke. Americans.

Back at my room, which I was sharing with Lek, I wondered in to find everyone enjoying more drinks. My entrance provoked laughter all round.

"What's so funny," I earnestly asked.

"Take a look at yourself in the mirror," somebody replied.

I did so, and immediately started laughing myself. My clothes were in shreds and my face covered in scratches. But aside from the throbbing lump on my head I was all right, so changed into some unshredded clothes and fixed myself a large drink and told the boys about my close encounter with death.

The next morning, I awoke to find I couldn't move my neck, which made playing drums very painful for at least the next three nights.

March 1982. After we found out that Ray Reneri had been stiffing us for years, we placed our US touring interests in the hands of Rainbow Talent Agency, who were based in Milwaukee. We'd done one tour with them, but this second tour turned out to be a disaster. The agency had told us that they had booked a good-sized tour of about forty shows, but we arrived in Milwaukee to pick up our travel expenses only to find out that they'd only booked ten shows.

Then, the president of Rainbow, Paul Edwards, told us that the agent that was dealing with us had disappeared a few days before, and had left no forwarding address. Paul didn't know much about the tour arrangements, but he said he'd do his best to find out what had happened.

It transpired that there were indeed ten solid shows, and thirty enquiries that had amounted to nothing. Of the ten shows booked, five venues had sent back a fifty percent advance, which – surprise, surprise – was nowhere to be found in the agency records or bank accounts.

After playing two of the scheduled shows, we decided to take the law into our own hands and make our own enquiries. We discovered that the agent in question had just got engaged, and that his new fiancée was in possession of a rather large engagement ring, and that he'd recently bought himself an orange Triumph Spitfire sports car, both, no doubt, funded by us.

After further investigations we found out where his girlfriend worked, and so decided to stakeout the building until he would inevitably arrive. We had time to kill.

The next morning found us sat in a car, a little down from her building, binoculars in hand, waiting for him to show his face. We kept a safe distance...we didn't want to scare him off before we could get our hands on him.

We already looked like we were in a heist movie, but what we didn't realise was that we'd been sat in a car for two hours, with binoculars, outside a bank. So, we were somewhat surprised when two police cars screeched up in front and behind us. Had we been real bank robbers, the game would have been up.

"Get out of the car slowly and put your hands above your heads," came the voice from one of the car's speakers.

We slowly obliged as two more cars pulled up, officers with guns drawn.

One officer eventually approached and demanded to know what we were doing sat outside a bank for two hours while looking at people through binoculars. I started to explain but he cut me off and instead took our ID back to his squad car.

Ten minutes later he returned, told us that our visas were in order, then explained that they'd been called because there was an armoured car that had waited for over an hour to pull up next to the bank, and had assumed that the car full of men was waiting for them. I finished explaining our story to the officer and asked if he could help. He declined, as it was a civil matter, but did inform us that there were two different offices on the same street for the company that employed the girlfriend of the agent we were looking for.

They advised us to not park outside banks, and left. Our ordeal had left us hungry (it was lunchtime, after all) so I volunteered to get burgers. As I got out of the car, an orange Spitfire pulled up outside the building we were watching, and the agent climbed out and entered the building. We followed him at a safe distance. He went into an office and kissed the receptionist…we didn't need to see the dirty great diamond on her finger to work that out.

We burst into the office, grabbed him and told him he was coming with us for questioning. We also requested the ring off the girlfriend, but she told us where to go and threatened to call the police and report us for kidnapping. Our plan had been to take him back to a club, whose owner we knew, to give him a good grilling, so I took the Spitfire keys off him and told the lads I'd follow them back to the club in the repossessed car.

We were on our way down the highway doing about 50mph when the traffic suddenly came to a halt. I slammed the brakes on and, to my eternal surprise, bugger all happened. I quickly swerved to the right. The lads looked at me as if I'd lost my mind as I flew past them on the inside.

"The brakes have gone!" I shouted out of the window.

I had to take evasive action or risk writing the Spitfire off, so, hitting the hard shoulder I used a combination of gears and handbrake to bring the vehicle to a stop. The boys followed me and asked me what was going on, to which I replied that the car was a death-trap, and that we should go much slower from here on.

We got to the club on the west side of Milwaukee and the owner arranged for us to go to a booth away from the regular drinkers where we could grill our agent. It didn't take long for him to admit that he'd taken the money, from which he'd bought the engagement ring and the Spitfire. We told him we were taking the car, and demanded the papers from him. He told us the documents were at the agency, so we called and arranged to have them dropped down to us. We also took his wallet, which contained a measly $200.

When the other agent turned up with the car's documents, we made an announcement in the bar that we were selling a sports car, but the customers were either too drunk, too poor, or both, to take it off our hands.

The club owner said he was interested in taking it for a test drive, so I warned him about the brakes. Ten minutes later he returned saying it wasn't worth much.

"I'll give you two hundred and fifty bucks for it," he muttered.

After about half an hour of haggling he had gone up to $450, which we also turned down.

"Four hundred and fifty dollars, a crate of Corona and a bottle of Yukon Jack," I suggested.

He pondered for a moment. We had a deal.

We allowed the rogue agent to call his girlfriend to give him a lift home. As we were about to leave, she arrived shouting and telling us what she thought of us. This provoked a smile in the agent, so Frank Renshaw head-butted him, dropping him to the floor where he rolled under the pool table. I pulled him out and slammed him against the wall and told him that if he ever used our name in connection with a show or any other kind of business, we would be back to see him.

Not long later we were driving south on Interstate ninety-four, the sun going down to our right. What better time to enjoy a Mexican beer and a Canadian liqueur?

We were due to play an afternoon concert at a county fair somewhere in the USA, and on our arrival to the back stage area we were informed that we were in a dry county...a dated and barbaric legality that prevents you from buying alcohol. This wouldn't do, we were pop stars and we had a reputation to uphold!

As we had a few hours to kill before the concert started, we decide to drive across to the next county that did sell alcohol, which we were told by a very friendly police officer was only 15 miles down the road. As he knew a short cut to a liquor store in the next county, he offered to escort us there, and we would follow him in our van. What a very helpful man. We found the store and all bought enough beer to last us through to the next day. As we set off to get back to the fair we asked if he would put on the blue flashing lights on his patrol car, which he happily did. I was driving the van behind the patrol car when I turned and smiled mischievously at the lads.

"Hold tight," I grinned, and put my foot down to the floor. We pulled out and overtook the patrol car at seventy miles-an-hour. The police officer gave chase in a scene that wouldn't have looked out of place in the Dukes of Hazard – wheels spinning and dust flying everywhere. When we arrived back at the fair the officer chastised me for my antics, but with a cold bottle of beer thrust into his hand, he calmed down somewhat. We have a great photo of him and his fellow officers arresting us against one of their patrol cars. The officer sent me the photo 20 years later.

Hamilton, Ontario, Canada. During a run there in the mid-eighties, we quickly discovered that there was nothing to do in the daytime apart from watch the strippers plying their trade in the same cabaret room that we performed in by night. One of those strippers had a room two doors down from me, and I got to spend a bit of time with her, but even more with her pet rat. I spent hours playing with him, often so long into the night that my sleep patterns were screwed up and I began to miss breakfast. On the third morning of missing breakfast, I decided to invest in a hot plate and frying pan, and bought some supplies of eggs, bacon, sausages, bread, mushrooms and tomatoes. I headed back to my room via the hotel restaurant and borrowed a plate, and a knife and fork. With one of everything bubbling away nicely in the frying pan, and with my mouth watering at the prospect, there was a knock at my door. With breakfast nearly cooked, I considered ignoring it, but it might have been important. So, I picked up the frying pan and answered the door with the pan in my hand. To my surprise, the hotel manageress was stood before me, arms crossed, and looking rather angry.

"Are you cooking in your room sir?" she asked, "as it violates our house rules and fire regulations."

I looked at the pan simmering in my hand, and looked back at her.

"No!" I quickly replied, slamming the door closed.

I quickly consumed my fry-up before she could return with a passkey. Twenty minutes later she banged on the door before letting herself in, by which time I had washed up and hidden my cooking equipment and food under the bed. The only thing I couldn't hide was the rich waft of a full English breakfast. After a few minutes of questioning me she left in a huff.

On one of our many tours of the USA we were on the road with Gerry and the Pacemakers, Billy J Kramer, Badfinger and the Troggs. It was August 1984 and, on this tour, I decided to buy a proper cooking set, which included a skillet, hot plate, two large pans and a large trunk to keep it all in. I bought the cooking gear from a pawnbroker, and the trunk from K-Mart. The whole lot cost me thirty dollars, but it meant culinary autonomy.

I had decided before embarking on this tour that I would make curries on our days off, so I had packed a few jars of curry paste in my suitcase before leaving for states. I had one jar of Vindaloo, one jar of Rogan Josh and a jar of Madras as well as a variety of spices. On the first night of the tour, we were staying in a Holiday Inn in downtown Chicago, so I put the word out to the rest of the lads in the Hermits that tonight was to be our first curry night. I went to a super market and picked up some minced meat, three pounds of steak, onions, tomato paste, Uncle Tom's rice and a selection of vegetables, not forgetting some six packs of Mexican beer. When I got back to the hotel it took me about an hour to get the dish bubbling, and while we drank some beers, I let it simmer for another hour.

In light of previous hotel room cooking experiences, I had taken the precaution of squeezing a bath mat under my door in order to stop the smell from escaping. My plan didn't work as the aroma of the curry found its way down several flights of stairs, through the reception and into the restaurant. It was when people in the restaurant started to ask what that fabulous smell was that the hotel manager began to investigate. I was told later that he had searched every floor looking for my curry kitchen. Maybe he wanted me to work in his kitchen?

By ten o'clock that night we'd feasted handsomely, and there was still plenty of curry left over. It was about this time when some of the lads in the other groups came back to their rooms after a drinking session in a local bar. Being half pissed and then smelling my spicy concoction drove them into frenzy, so they started banging on doors in search of curry. Every last bit was devoured, and curry night became a regular feature of that tour.

One night in a Holiday Inn, somewhere in the USA, I decided to retire early. That probably meant it was about 2am. Once in my room, I poured a large slug of whisky for a nightcap and turned on the TV. I relaxed so effectively that I woke up at the table sometime later, with the whisky bottle half empty and my bladder rather full. In my sleepy daze, I mistook the adjoining room door for the bathroom, entered the darkened room, then made my way to a narrow crack of light coming from beneath the bathroom door. I was halfway through doing my business when I saw two women run past me through the mirror. 'That's a bit strange' I thought, and carried on relieving myself.

Then, a uniformed man appeared over my shoulder and asked me what I was doing.

"I'm having a piss," I replied, 'who the bloody hell are you?"

He told me he was hotel security and that I needed to leave the bathroom immediately, so I hastily finished what I was doing before he asked me to step into the corridor with him.

"Is this your room?" he asked me.

"Of course, it is," I replied.

"Please show me your key, sir?" I obliged. "Now, please look at the number on your key, sir, then look at the number on this door. I think you'll find they're different."

In my sleepy/half drunken disposition I studied the key fob and the door, and sure enough my key said 489, and the door 487. Then I noticed the two women stood in the corridor in their nighties. I looked back into the room and I could see the light coming through the adjoining door, and quickly realized what I'd done. I apologized profusely, and timidly made my way back to my own room, but not before the security officer had locked the adjoining door from both sides.

As I dozed off in bed, I could hear laughter coming from the next room, and counted myself lucky that they'd woken up…had they not, there's every chance I could have climbed into one of their beds, and found myself in bigger trouble.

The next morning, I waited until the last moment before they closed the breakfast room, and coyly sat in the corner behind a newspaper. The thought of seeing the two women again filled me with dread.

1985. Keith Rose was a very good friend of mine who I first met at my local pub, The High Grove in Gatley, many years ago. He was a painter and decorator at the time and a very funny fellow indeed as he had the same sense of fun as me. Once in a while we would need somebody to drive us to a show or just to help out with setting our gear up on stage. On one occasion we asked him to go to Germany with us for a two-week tour of one-night stands across the whole country. On one of these nights, we were playing in Stuttgart, but our hotel was in Frankfurt. We were based in Frankfurt in the same hotel for about four days, as it was easier to stay in one place than move into different hotels each day, so when we finished the show in Stuttgart, Keith had to drive us back to Frankfurt, which was only about a two-hour drive.

As was standard in those days, we all bought a load of German beers to keep us company on the drive back. When we arrived at the outskirts of Frankfurt we drove into a thick fog, so dense that you couldn't see past the front of the van. Keith did his best, but within a few minutes we were utterly lost somewhere in the suburbs of Frankfurt, although the four of us didn't care much as we were fairly pissed by this point. Keith drove and drove, just looking for a sign that would take us into the Centre of the city where our hotel was. All of a sudden he braked sharply to avoid going into the back of a tram. The only damage was a little beer, split onto the floor of the van. As the tram moved away, Keith looked up to see that the tram had 'Frankfurt Centrum' lit up on the back. 'Follow that tram' was the cry, so Keith did his best to keep the back of the tram in our sights. In our collective wisdom we had decided that a tram wouldn't get lost because it travels on tracks – we would soon be home.

Just then, the fog cleared and we all gaped out of the windows to discover we were inside the largest building any of us had ever seen; it was the tram terminal. Keith was laughing so much that he'd forgotten how we'd got into the terminal, so spent the next five minutes looking for an opening that we could escape from. Some of the tram drivers were not amused by our presence, and I'm sure that some of them were swearing in German at us to get the hell out of their building. Eventually we found our way out of the terminal, and a few minutes later we were safely back in our Frankfurt hotel.

Paul Farnell was in the band on bass guitar from 1982-89, and when touring, I often shared a room with him. The trouble with Paul was that he snored – persistently and very loudly. After three weeks into a USA tour, I was getting hardly any good sleep as I was woken up every half an hour by his phenomenal snoring. Before going to bed each night, I would make a pile of items – shoes, books, a hair brush, toilet rolls etc. – by my side of my bed, just so I had something to throw at him, and hopefully stop the snoring for a while. After another night of interrupted sleep, I decided that drastic measures were needed, so after breakfast I went shopping for something to solve the problem. After a few hours of shopping, I ended up in a second-hand shop in downtown Cleveland, Ohio, and I found the very thing to stop him snoring. It was a chainsaw, and it was mine for the princely sum of $45.00, plus tax.

The very next night when he started to snore, I was ready with my supplies of missiles, and as a last resort, my new chainsaw. After going through my missiles the snoring hadn't stopped, so 'this is it', I had said to myself, he's asked for it. I located the tool, which I had already removed the chain from, and filled it with petrol. I went over to the curtains and opened them a little bit so that when he woke up he would be confronted by a startling view, and would be able to see what I had in my hands. I stood over him, started the engine, and allowed the saw to roar into life. He looked up in horror and saw the insane look on my face before noticing the chainsaw in my hand. He let out a scream that was almost as loud as my chain saw, and froze in terror as I worked the chain saw across his throat. I held it there until he realized his head was still where it was supposed it be. Eventually I cut the engine and he stopped screaming, the room now deadly quiet and full of blue smoke. I looked down at him with a mad glint in my eyes and said that if he ever woke me up again, I would put the chain next time. I got back into bed just as the phone rang; it was the hotel receptionist saying that there had been a complaint about noise and the sound of screaming coming from our room. I said that I had heard it too and put the phone down, rolled over and the best sleep I'd had in weeks. Paul never woke me up again on that tour as I think he was too frightened to go to sleep.

The next time I ever heard him snore was one night when the rest of the group were playing poker in our room. We had a table at the end of his bed and were into a serious game of poker when he started rattling the windows. The other guys were amazed at the volume and asked me how I put up with the bloody noise. I said that this was the first time in a while, and told them the story of the chainsaw. On this occasion I slipped a piece of tissue paper down between two of his toes, took out my lighter and lit the paper. The other guys protested with alarm as Paul let out another blood-curdling scream, but I just adopted a crazed look and shouted: "it's time for more treatment!"

The other guys left very soon after that and vowed they'd never share a room with me. In fact, for the rest of that tour, I got a room to myself. I still have the chainsaw, which has been very useful deforesting my garden in Manchester.

On New Year's Eve, 1985, an American promoter called David Fishof came to see us at the Crest Hotel in Southampton, where we were performing. He liked the show and asked us if we would like to tour the USA the next year on The Monkees 20th Anniversary Tour, along with Gary Puckett, and The Grass Roots. We worked out a deal and we were all set to start in May 1986. The rehearsals for the show were at the Concord Hotel, a very large Hotel complex with a theatre and rehearsal rooms, set on Kiamesha Lake in the Catskill Mountains, New York State.

When we arrived in New York we went to the same car rental place in New Jersey that we went to for every American tour. This time we hired a Chevrolet Caprice, which, at the time, was the largest station wagon ever built, and after a number of altercations with a variety of wildlife on our way upstate, the vehicle was quickly christened 'The Deer Hunter'.

The promoter had done a fantastic job promoting the tour. His office in New York was next door to Screen Gems who owned the Monkees Logo, which he leased for a year. A week before the tour started, he paid MTV to host a full weekend showing old Monkees TV shows non-stop. Young teenage girls in the USA, who had never seen the Monkees first time round, thought this was a new boy band, not realising that the band had hit the big time twenty years earlier.

The line-up was three-quarters of that outfit that had burst into the charts and onto TV screens in 1966 – Davy Jones, Mickey Dolenz and Peter Tork. Michael Nesmith had left the band in 1970 and was too busy doing his own things to be coaxed back for the tour. Incidentally, Nesmith's Mother, Bette Nesmith Graham (who was a secretary), had invented Liquid Paper in the fifties. When she died in 1980, Michael inherited half of her estate – a cool $50 million, so he really didn't need the money.

The Monkees had a nine-piece band, which included a brass section – a group of superb young musicians from the Juilliard School in New York with whom we got on extremely well from the start. In fact, we got on very well with everybody involved with the tour…it was a very enjoyable dynamic to be a part of. The first show, on the 24th May 1986, was at The Concord Hotel Complex. The show was well received and we went on to The Tropicana, Atlantic City for a three-day engagement that took us into June. We were doing six shows a week and after two weeks David Fishof, the promoter, came to us said he would like to extend the tour a further six weeks, we of course we agreed to. Lek telephoned Brian Gannon, our UK agent, and asked him to move any shows in the UK to later in the year.

Also, David told us that he was now booking venues that would hold ten thousand fans or more. After three weeks on the road, The Monkees, who were traveling in three separate Winnebago motor homes, decided to rent three Stage

Coaches. That's a term for large bus with a lounge at the front and rear sleeping quarters. The crew also had their own, even though all eight of them had to share it. I have to say that they were the best road crew I have ever had the pleasure to work with. We were still travelled in our Deer Hunter, which was equipped with a radar detector and CB radio, meaning we could travel around 90mph without getting speeding tickets. It also meant that we could leave our hotel an hour later, and arrive at the next hotel an hour before the rest of the tour as their buses could only manage a stately 55mph.

Once the first six weeks were out of the way we began playing large arenas with a ten thousand or so capacity, and we were selling out nearly all of them. The Monkees merchandising machine was incredible. They had a truckload of goods, from T-Shirts to programmes and everything else Monkees-related you can imagine, all delivered to the venues each day. Unfortunately, because of contractual agreements, the rest of the bands weren't allowed to sell their own merchandise, allowing The Monkees to clean up a lot of extra revenue. The bands' riders were quite generous. Our rider consisted of a case of Corona beer, a bottle of red wine, a bottle white wine, a bottle Scotch and a bottle Vodka plus a variety of snacks and a hot meal every day. Gone were the days of partying all night with The Who – we could no longer maintain those levels of alcohol consumption – so, invariably, the crew were invited to our dressing room to help themselves to our grog.

Music Industry Insight #137: The three Monkees were on a different pay structure to each other. Davy Jones had the most generous contract, followed by Mickey Dolenz and then Peter Tork, such was the pecking-order in terms of popularity. Whenever one of them went to David Fishof for an increase in money the other two would find out, a big argument would ensue, then the Promoter would have to increase the other two's pay. Half way through the second extension David Fishof asked all the bands to do another six weeks, and everybody apart from Davy Jones agreed to the terms. Davy told the promoter he wanted more money and would not negotiate until he'd arranged for a red Porsche to be delivered to his mother's house in the UK within twenty-four hours. Davy even gave the Promoter the specifications of the model he wanted. The next day, the promoter came to Davy's dressing room to negotiate another six weeks wages. Davey told him to hang on while he made a telephone call to his mother. He asked his mother to look out of the front window of her house and to tell him what she saw. She said that someone had left a red sports car on the drive. Davy told his Mum that car was his and not to worry. Davy ended the call and deal was safe.

After eight weeks on the road and playing shows six nights a week and traveling thousands of miles in the Deer Hunter, I was up to my usual tricks, mainly with the crew. One day, at the Jack Murphy Stadium, San Diego, California, Mark Narramore, one of the lighting engineers was adjusting a spotlight high up above the stage. The only way to reach the lighting gantry was by using a wire ladder at the side of the stage, which could be lowered and raised with a rope. While he was up there, I decided to raise the wire ladder and tie it off. I left him up there for about an hour before I untied the rope so the ladder was released and he could come down. When he came down, I was laughing at my work when he smiled and promised that he would get me back. It didn't take long; the next day he came up behind me and gave a bear hug, and inadvertently cracked two of my ribs. When I eventually got my breath back, I smiled and said: "This is war".

A few weeks later we were driving towards Wisconsin and noticed a firework outlet just off Interstate 90, and what with our famous love affair with incendiaries, naturally we pulled off the highway and headed straight in through the door. I purchased a variety of fireworks, along with the biggest rip-rap (Jumping Jack) they had on offer, which happened to be about the size of a shoe box. The next day we were playing Dane County Coliseum, Madison, Wisconsin, and we had a very large dressing room with four toilet cubicles in a row. It was an hour before show time and most of the crew were chatting to us along with Gary Puckett and Rob Grill of the Grass Roots. When anybody from the crew came into the Hermits dressing room to eat and drink, they were always polite enough to ask first. We were all standing around having a laugh and telling jokes when Mark Narramore came into the room, helped himself to a large sandwich, and strolled through into the toilet. Payback time! I rushed to my gig bag and brought out the huge firework that I'd bought the day before. I lit it, advised everybody to put their fingers in their ears, and pushed it under the toilet door. Within a couple of seconds, it sounded like a thousand bangers were going off, and in such a confined space the volume of the explosions was phenomenal. After a minute a dishevelled looking Mark came out of the toilet, his cloths gently smoking, and covered in red and white confetti from the firework. He merely looked at me and silently walked out of the dressing room. The expression on his face was of sheer terror. Game set and match to me, I think. I found out years later from Mark, that he was having a piss when the rip-rap came under the toilet door. He said he'd jumped onto the toilet seat while still pissing, but had to cover his crotch to protect his manhood, so not only could he not put his fingers in his ears, but he ended up with piss all over his hands and underpants.

Pat, my fiancé, came out from the UK to join me on the tour three times. The second time was when we played at the Hilton Hotel, Las Vegas. We arrived late and checked in around 11.00pm. After I'd filled out the registration form the receptionist informed me that we had two hundred dollars a day 'per diem'. I asked her when the 'per diem' began, and she said it expired at midnight. It was now 11.15pm. As quickly as possible, Pat and I rushed to our suite and ordered a lobster for Pat and I ordered Alaskan King Crab Legs, as well as a bottle of Johnnie Walker and a bottle Brandy. It was quite a supper.

We then had twenty minutes left to spend the rest of the allowance, which was around one hundred dollars. We went straight down to the main bar and were greeted by most of the crew. I explained the situation to them and, because the crew did not have an allowance, I ordered several rounds of drinks for them until that day's allowance ran out.

In Las Vegas casinos, no show could ever run over one and a half hours, so Herman's Hermits, Gary Puckett and The Grass Roots had twelve and a half minutes each, with a forty-five second change over between acts – totalling forty minutes – leaving The Monkees fifty minutes. We'd had to rehearse the changeovers in our spare time before the first night to ensure The Monkees weren't forced to shorten their set. Two days later as Pat and I were sun bathing by the pool, Pat saw me pinch myself and laugh and I had to explain that I was just making sure I hadn't died and gone to Heaven, as we had two hundred Dollars to spend daily on food and drink, only had to play twelve and half minutes per show, and we were staying at the Las Vegas Hilton on the Executive Top Floor (with our own lift) for the week, not to mention being paid. Not a bad gig.

My fortieth birthday fell during this tour, and Pat came out to help me celebrate. After we'd played a show at Cape Cod Melody Tent, Hyannis, Massachusetts, we had a wonderful party. Everybody from the tour was there, the drink flowed freely and we had a wonderful time, including our customary cake fight, the damage for which had to be paid to the hotel as we checked out, roughly 3 hours later, very short on sleep, in order to drive to New York.

One of the best jokes I ever pulled was on John Leslie, the saxophonist for The Monkees. It happened in New Orleans at The Superdome. John was telling me that he got arrested in the French Quarter on a night off from the tour for drinking beer out of a glass in the street. In New Orleans, it's OK to drink out of a plastic container in public, but not a glass one. The backstage area at the Superdome was one large room, which was partitioned off into six different sections and passed for dressing rooms. In the intermission, while The Monkees were getting ready for show time, I noticed two police officers standing guard outside the dressing area. I went up to them and asked if they were up for playing a joke on one of The Monkees band, and they were as keen as me. I told them what had happened to John the night before to their great delight. Without hesitation they went straight into the Monkees dressing area and called out: "Mr John Leslie make yourself known". John put his hand up and they walked up to him, spun him around and handcuffed him. You could hear a pin drop as they told him they were taking him back to the police station where he had been arrested the night before, as the paper work was not correct. With that they marched him out to their patrol car. The Monkees' tour manager was following behind them protesting that they mustn't take him away as he was due on stage in five minutes. I was following them with my camera in hand waiting for the right moment, which came as they threw him into the back of the patrol car. John was as white as a sheet when I took the photo. He almost fainted as the officers took the handcuffs off him and told him he was free to go. John looked at me.

"Gotcha," I said, as I took another photo.

I was the only one who knew what was going on and had to admit I thought I had gone too far that time, but the next day apparently, I became a living legend for my joking around - not my drumming.

The Deer Hunter was a very fast vehicle. It could cruise comfortably at 100mph on the interstate highway with no trouble at all. As I mentioned before, we had a radar detector and CB radio in the car, but that still didn't stop Lek from getting a ridiculous number of speeding tickets. On one occasion Lek was driving North – or should I say 'flying' up Interstate 75 towards Tallahassee – when the Radar detector went off at full volume, meaning there was a patrol car very nearby. Lek hit the brakes, and as I looked out of the passenger window, I could see a State Trooper patrol car on the other side of the highway.

The patrol car instantly put on its red and blue flashing lights, and attempted to cross over to our side of the highway. In America nearly all the interstate highways have a median – a central grass division between both sides – and looking in the mirror, I could see that the patrol car was about half a mile behind by the time it had manoeuvred its way onto our side of the highway. I told Lek there was a junction coming up where the 75 splits with 275, and told him to take the 75 North to St Petersburg, but not to indicate. After a few minutes there was no sign of the patrol car, so we gunned it back to the junction at nearly 100mph again. Twenty minutes later the radar detector went off again but there were no police in sight.

However, when I looked in the mirror, there was the State Trooper right behind us, lit up like a Christmas tree. Lek pulled over to the hard shoulder and stopped. The Trooper told Lek to open his window and show the vehicle registration papers and his driving licence. The patrol officer told Lek that he had seen the front of the car drop as Lek hit the brakes some miles back. The patrol officer was very pleasant at first as he told us that it had taken him twenty minutes to catch up with us, to which Lek replied: "Yes they don't make these police cars like they used to".

Immediately the officer took out his citation wallet and wrote Lek a ticket for doing 95mph in a 55mph zone and gave him an $80 fine. The officer was really rather kind to us. He said he knew we going over 100mph but decided to let us off with just 95mph. He also said if he wanted to, he could put Lek in jail and have a court hearing the next day. It was another lucky escape for the Deer Hunter…one of many.

The tour continued until late November for Herman's Hermits, and we had completed over one hundred and eighty shows. We then had to get to Germany for a three-week tour, which had been booked through Hainer Hass, one of the biggest agents in Germany, not to mention a good friend of the band. I could write another book about all the things that happened on that tour.

In the spring of 1989, following tours of Australia/New Zealand and Scandinavia, Herman's Hermits underwent a double personnel change. Leaving, were Paul Farnell and lead singer/rhythm guitarist Garth Elliott, who had joined the band at the same time as Paul. Filling their boots were fellow Mancunians Rod Gerrard and Geoff Foot, who incidentally wrote Herman's Hermits' 1971 single 'She's a Lady'. Both Rod and Geoff were strong vocally, so lead vocal duties were split, and harmonies were bolstered. After an intensive rehearsal period, on 12th June 1989 we flew to the States to headline the 30th Anniversary of Rock 'n' Roll tour, which would keep us busy for three months. Also on the tour were Tiny Tim, Otis Day & the Knights, Chuck Negron (former lead singer of Three Dog Night), The Coasters featuring Cornell Gunter, Mike Pinera (former lead singer of Blues Image and Iron Butterfly), Al Wilson, Donnie Brooks, Cannibal & the Headhunters, and The Troggs.

We had a nice Independence Day treat on 4th July in Austin, Texas, where Jerry Lee Lewis took the headline slot. We also managed to get some studio time backing Tiny Tim on a record, before flying back to the UK to tour with The Byrds and our old friends The Merseybeats.

10

The 1990s – the reinvention of Britpop

1990 was another year of large tours: first off was a two-week tour of the USA starting on the 5th March at Arizona Charlie's in Las Vegas, and winding up at the Firehouse in Salisbury, Maryland on the 17th. While we were down on the Mexican border we met some military aircrew in a bar after our show at The Imperial Valley Fair, and they invited us to watch the Blue Arrow practise at a US Air Force base nearby. I actually got to sit in an A18 fighter on condition I didn't touch any of the buttons, which, of course, I resisted!

On our return to the UK, we immediately began a long tour of Germany and the UK, then in July set off back to the States for an even longer tour. Many of the dates were at casinos and state fairs, including those of Wisconsin, Iowa, New Jersey, and Florida.

After a two-week engagement at the Eldorado Casino in Reno in July, we had a few days off and decided to make our umpteenth visit to the Grand Canyon as two of the band hadn't seen it. By the time we'd got to the entrance of the national park it was already dark, so we decided to have a meal and do the canyon the following morning. We had booked a motel nearby, in fact, it was the only one with any rooms available for about 100 miles. But that didn't stop it being horrendously busy.

In the hotel's only restaurant, we were behind about two hundred other hungry people, all vying for the attention of just two waitresses. We eventually got served and all ordered soup followed by chicken and chips, all except for Lek, who ordered a bowl of chilli and portion of chips, thinking it might be a quicker, therefore, simpler choice. Apparently, this was not the case.

After ten or fifteen minutes our soups arrived, but nothing for Lek. The waitress came back and removed our soup bowls, so Lek enquired about his chilli and chips.

"It'll be right out," she replied.

Next, our chicken and chips arrived. Naturally, I wound Lek up a little by suggesting that he should have ordered the same as us, and by telling him just how good the chicken was. He shouted the waitress over and asked where his chilli and chips were.

"They'll be right out," she repeated.

Ten minutes later she came out with his portion of chips. As he finished eating them, she arrived with his bowl of chilli. He then told her that he wanted chips at the same time as chilli, and persuaded her to fetch more chips. As she disappeared into the kitchen, he discovered his chilli was cold. With a little help from me, Lek is now getting visibly agitated.

The waitress returned with more chips, but Lek informs her that the chilli is cold, and that she would have to take it back to the kitchen to reheat it. After another indeterminable amount of time, she returned and placed the chilli in front of him.

"Wait there while I test the chilli," he said, picking up his spoon. After a moment he slams the spoon down onto the table and loudly declares that the chilli is "still fucking cold", and that he'd eaten all of his chips.

The waitress had admirable control to not get upset or agitated, and calmly informed Lek that she'd be right back with his chilli and chips. Before she left, just to complicate matters, we all requested separate bills.

We passed the next ten minutes by really laying into Lek, how good the chicken had been, hadn't it been the best bowl of soup you've ever tasted?

We'd now been in the restaurant for just over an hour when the chilli appeared for the third time. The waitress placed the bowl in front of Lek and made good her escape before he could test it.

"Argh!" he bellowed, after taking a spoonful. He picked up the bowl of chilli, marched into the kitchen and threw the bowl of chilli at the wall.

"One hour and still cold fucking chilli!" we could hear him shout.

He strode out of the kitchen and shouted at us not to pay any more of the bill. The entire restaurant was under a deadly hush, nobody daring to make eye contact with Lek as he stormed out.

When we got back to the motel, he bought a packed of potato chips from a vending machine, whilst trying to convince me that he wasn't very hungry anyway. I'm certain that if I'd laughed at that point, he would have killed me in the night.

The next day we were doing the tourist bit, taking photos by the canyon's edge when Lek, 'Mr Angry' as Geoff called him sometimes, somewhat forthrightly asked Geoff to take a photo of him. He gave Geoff his camera (which Geoff was really not sure how to use) and assumed his pose, but Geoff just studied the camera in his confusion.

"Come on, are you fucking new?" barked Lek, "just press the fucking button and get on with it!"

Geoff panicked, took a look through the viewfinder, and hastily pressed a button. Unfortunately, he pressed the button that rewinds the film back to the beginning. Geoff couldn't give the camera back to Lek while it was making this noise so he pretended he was lining up another picture, with all the swagger of a professional photographer.

"Have you taken the fucking photo or what?" shouted Lek, just as the rewind process finished, at which point he handed back the camera.

Geoff never told Lek what had happened, as he knew he would get the third degree.

Just after he handed the camera back, a gust of wind blew Lek's hat over the edge of the canyon. That did it for Lek, and he shouted at Steve Quirk, our roadie, to go down and get his hat, and to be quick about it. We all walked to the edge to watch Steve climb down about fifty feet to where the hat had come to rest in some brush. Steve was a pretty fit guy and had no trouble scaling down the wall of the canyon to retrieve Lek's hat, but when he got back to the top, he had a variety of scrapes and small cuts on his legs. The rest of the day passed without incident and we were back at our hotel by seven that night, just in time for the three-dollar buffet and a drink or two. The next night in the ballroom, Steve said he didn't feel that good and went straight to his room after the show. The day after he stayed in bed for the duration, only to come down at show time, and he looked terrible…his face was red, he was sweating, and his legs were swollen, so we told him to go back to his room and sent a doctor to see him.

    The next day he said he was going back to New Jersey, where he lived with his girlfriend, to see his own doctor. When he got off the plane at Newark he went straight to hospital where he was admitted immediately and put on a drip. The doctors were baffled as to what had caused his condition. They asked Steve if he had any allergies to anything or if he had done anything out of the ordinary. He told them that he'd cut his legs in the Grand Canyon while retrieving a hat. They suspected he might have been bitten by something like a spider, a mosquito, or possibly a small snake. Steve went downhill very fast. By the next night a priest had read him the last rites, so the doctors gave him a cocktail of antibiotics, antihistamines and various other drugs. Whatever they gave him worked and no doubt saved his life, but he did have to use walking sticks for several weeks. He didn't come back onto the road that tour.

The last week of the tour was spent playing on the S.S. Caribe and Pat came out to join us as we cruised from Miami to Grand Cayman, Jamaica, Cancun, Playa del Carmen, and Cozumel, before returning to Miami. This last stretch of the cruise took us through the tail end of a hurricane. We managed to fulfil our contract on our final show, but came on stage in life jackets and did our best to play as the microphones and my drum kit slid around the stage. A show to remember but the audience loved it. The low point was, by the time we finished, all bars on board were closed with bottles, glasses etc., taken down and locked safely away.

Life on the road with Herman's Hermits can really take its toll, and in March of 1991 Geoff Foot decided to leave the band to spend more time with his wife and family. This left a big hole in the group, and as somebody with his ability as lead singer, frontman and bass player, a replacement would be hard to find. Lek and I advertised for a replacement bass player/lead singer, but it's very hard to find somebody in the right age bracket that is willing to travel the world and be away from home so much. In the end we found a bass player and singer by the name of Keith Roberts, who was playing a solo gig in a pub called The Manchester Arms.

We had just two weeks rehearsals before we were back on the road doing some shows in the UK, and then in mid-April we had another tour of the U.S.A., which ran until the second week of June. Then, with just five days off we were back on the road to Germany, Switzerland and Austria to tour with The Tremeloes, Showaddywaddy, The Rubettes, The

Searchers, The Equals, Chris Andrews, and Desmond Dekker and The Aces.

We spent the next few months zigzagging the globe before returning to London on 11th October where we were booked to play on a sixties Festival at Wembley Conference and Exhibition Centre. Many sixties' acts were there including The Bruvvers and Mike Berry. Rod Gerrard and Keith Roberts, who shared the lead vocals for us, had both contracted laryngitis, so Karl Green, our original bass player and singer very kindly offered to stand in as lead singer. Herman's Hermits went down a storm thanks to Karl saving the day.

The high point of that year was doing a Greek TV show called The Rock & Roll Party on New Year's Eve. The bill was fantastic - The Shirelles, Neil Sedaka, Lovin' Spoonful, the Mamas & Papas, Dion, Paul Revere & The Raiders, Davy Jones, The Platters and many, many more. We were due to play five songs live at around eleven o'clock, but there been some technical problems and the show was delayed by about an hour. We eventually went on just after midnight and brought the house down. Apparently, Neil Sedaka had made an agreement with the TV Company that he would go just after midnight, so wasn't very pleased at all when we went on the stage at exactly the time he was supposed to be going home. In the end, he went on just after one o'clock in the morning. Well…that's show business.

At the beginning of 1992, Lek, Tony Mansfield, Mike Maxfield and myself formed a promotion company called

Rockerama for the purpose of promoting shows. Our first show was at Quaffers Night Club in Stockport. The bill was Herman's Hermits, The Olympics with Johnny Peters, The Dakotas, Dave Berry and The Cruisers, Freddie and The Dreamers, and The Emperors of Rhythm. We also invited original Hermits Karl Green and Keith Hopwood to join us on stage. The show was on the 19th of March was a sell out with about 1400 happy punters in the audience. On the 20th March, the next day, we were in Paris to do a French TV show with Keith Hopwood deputizing for Lek who was having chemotherapy and was advised not to fly – we did several shows in March with Keith standing in for Lek. Early April we caught a ferry to Sweden with the Dakotas for a three-week tour. Lek was still receiving chemotherapy for Non-Hodgkin's Lymphoma, so, deputising for him was Graham Lee, nicknamed Monty. On the second morning of the tour, a photo-shoot was organised by the promoter just before we left for the next engagement. The Dakotas and Herman's Hermits formed a line for the photographer to take the photo, then, he asked us not to move so that he could take our names. He went down the line asking our names. When he got to Monty and asked for his name, Monty replied: "no, I'm only depping". The photographer moved on and gathered the rest of the information he needed. The next morning, the Swedish national paper featured our photo with a story of what we were doing over there. Under the photo where our names were noted, Monty's name appeared as 'Moany Depping', which provided a great deal of laughter at his expense. When the laughter stopped, we got into the bus and drove two hundred miles to the next town. Checking into our next hotel, I noticed Monty looking a bit confused. When asked what the matter was, he said he couldn't find his suitcase. I asked him if he'd loaded into the bus before we left the last town, to which he said no. "There's your answer right there then, it's still at the last hotel," I replied. As Lek would say: "are you new or what?" Everybody that was a similar size to Monty lent him clothes to wear until he got his suitcase back about a week later.

During the tour we played at a club in Sundsvall, a nice city on the east coast of Sweden. We would play two shows there, with a week between performances. The club had accommodation for five people in one large room, so it was decided that The Dakotas would stay at the club while we boarded at a small hotel in the city. The hotel was bleak and cold. The breakfast consisted of a small piece of cheese wrapped in plastic, biscuits wrapped in plastic and a knob of butter wrapped in plastic, which was solid because the rooms were freezing. I told the boys to tell The Dakotas that we had a full English breakfast and that the hotel was fantastic. They told us that the bar had closed as soon as the show finished, and that they'd had no breakfast. Two days later Eddie Mooney, the lead singer of The Dakotas, said he'd like to have a word with me about the accommodation situation the next time we were back at the club. He suggested that it was The Dakotas' turn to stay at the nice hotel that we'd stayed in the week before. I said he was right and that it was only fair that the Hermits stayed at the club for the night. Five days later we were back in Sundsvall for the return performance at the club.

The show went great to another sell out audience and after the show The Dakotas went on their way to the hotel we'd stayed in, having to cart their luggage in, in what had become very heavy snow. Meantime, I had a few words with the manager of the club and the beers started to flow. We kept the bar open for a few hours, and a good time was had by all, especially when the manager said that a full English breakfast will be served at ten the next morning. At eleven o'clock The Dakotas arrived back at the club for our departure to the next town. They came in from the freezing weather to the smell of eggs, bacon, mushrooms, toast and fresh coffee. They couldn't believe their eyes when they saw all the empty plates on the table. Eddie Mooney came up to me and said the hotel was terrible and they had a plastic breakfast. I told him they should have stayed at the club, as the bar was open until late. I was on form the whole tour, putting one over on the Dakotas at every opportunity. On the last day of the tour Eddie told me he'd bought a blue movie to take back to England. I told him I wouldn't allow him take a blue movie in the bus we were traveling in. I told him that if customs officers found it, it would be detrimental to Herman's Hermits' image, so, believing me, he dumped it in a bin.

The first quarter of 1993 saw us doing more package shows with other sixties groups. January 1st Westfalenhallen in Dortmund we were on an Oldie Festival show with Suzy Quatro, Middle Of The Road, The Tremeloes, Slade, Dave Dee, The Rubettes, Showaddywaddy, Bay City Rollers and The Mamas And Papas. It was official – we were now 'oldies!

Other shows during this period saw us team up with acts such as Freddie & The Dreamers, The Foundations, Tommy Bruce & The Bruisers, Pinkertons's Colours, The Troggs, The Swinging Blue Jeans, The Rocking Berries, Marmalade, The Fortunes, Mike Pender's Searchers, Ricky Valance, Steve Ellis & Love Affair, Dave Berry, Dozy Beaky Mick & Tich, Wayne Fontana and The Mindbenders, and The Foundations with Clem Curtis. It was nice to be on the road meeting so many of the bands that we toured with so often in the sixties. Knowing most of the guys in these groups meant we would meet up in a bar after the show and have a drink, tell the latest jokes, and catch up on all the gossip.

At the end of April, we were back in Las Vegas doing a two-week run at The Four Queens, then moving on to Reno for a two-week engagement at The El Dorado Casino. Friday nights in the Casino restaurants were fabulous as it was usually fish night and all you can eat. Alaskan king crab legs were always on the buffet along with New Zealand mussels and oysters. We had a week of one-nighters then back home for some shows in Germany and the UK, only to return to the US a few weeks later for another tour, and a meet up with Jeff Hanlon, who used to be our UK road manager in the late sixties. He was managing Gary Glitter, and had been for several years, and on a few occasions, Jeff had invited Pat and I to his shows in Manchester. We met up with Jeff in Madison, Wisconsin, where he was recording with Gary in a studio there. Jeff asked us if we wanted to put some vocals and hand clapping on the track that was going to be Gary's next single in the States, which we were happy to do. This was a few years before Gary's troubles, and the irreparable damage to his reputation. The session went great and afterwards we went out for dinner with Gary and Jeff, whose 50th birthday it was. When the stories about Gary became news, the record was obviously shelved.

Between 1991 and 1993, the band, under Lek and Rod Gerrard's creative influence, had been putting together new material of a country rock/rockabilly style. Rod had written some good songs about our times on the road in the USA, but the public did not except the change in Herman's Hermits' musical style. The crossover was too much, in spite of having some very snazzy country and western shirts made for our publicity photos. The proposed album title was Back Home, but remains unissued.

1994 was a horrendous year for Herman's Hermit. We began the year on the usual merry-go-round of tours and TV shows. Then in March we did a show at a sixties weekend at Butlins in Minehead, Somerset, where played half a show of Herman's Hermits hits, and the other half the country/rockabilly material that we'd been working on. When we finished the show, the stage manager came up to me and said: "What was all that country shit about?" Maybe it was time to rethink our direction.

In May we were booked on three-week tour of the north-western United States. Lek, who had been diagnosed with Non-Hodgkin Lymphoma, was very ill and shouldn't have done this tour, but he insisted on going on it. He was told by his doctors that flying that many flights would deplete the white blood corpuscles in the body, and as the trip was over six thousand miles, he would need to see a specialist and get a white blood corpuscles top-up as soon as possible after arriving in the States. The day after we arrived, he saw a specialist and was given his treatment, and the tour began. Everything was fine for about ten days, although he tired very quickly. Leonie, Lek's wife, was with him on this tour, and in retrospect should have said enough was enough, and taken him to a hospital for more treatment before taking him home. We were on tour with another group who had a solid lead guitarist who could easily have covered for Lek, but he insisted on carrying on and completing the tour. The last show Lek was to play was an open-air show in Moses Lake, near Seattle, WA. He had to sit down on a stool just to get through the show, and he had an electric fire next to him on the stage to keep warm. Two days before the last show I went to Lek's hotel room to see how he was holding up, but he couldn't speak. I asked him if he fancied his favourite meal – calves' liver with onions and mashed potatoes – but he just smiled, which I took as a yes. I searched restaurant after restaurant until I found one that served calves liver and onion with mashed potatoes as a take away. When I finally got back to the hotel, I just put the meal down in front of him and left the room. Leonie told me later that he ate the whole meal. In hindsight, I wish I'd got myself one.

The day after the last show in Moses Lake, we were booked on a flight back from Seattle to Manchester, which is a long flight, and Lek was very ill by now. When we arrived at Manchester Airport on the Wednesday morning, Leonie had organized a wheelchair for Lek to be taken off the plane. She took him home then went straight to Christies Hospital in Withington, Manchester. Derek Leckenby died in the early hours of Saturday 4th June of pneumonia…his two-year battle with Non-Hodgkin Lymphoma was over.

We were booked to appear in Berlin on Saturday evening for an open-air concert and TV show, so on the Wednesday afternoon I phoned Keith Hopwood to see if he was available to stand in for Lek, which he was. Lek always said the show must go on, no matter what happens. I got the phone call from Leonie around 3am on that Saturday morning, letting me know that Lek had passed away in the night. By 10am we were at Manchester airport waiting to board a plane to Berlin. When we arrived in Berlin we were met and driven to a hotel to freshen up, and then on to the concert, where more than ten thousand people were waiting for the show to start. There were a lot of English bands on the show and they had all heard the news about Lek passing away, and one by one came to offer their condolences. It was hard doing the show that night, but we got through somehow. Top of the bill was Steppenwolf, a Canadian-American rock band. Their road crew took forty-five minutes to reset the stage, which was about forty minutes too long. After their second song most of the audience decided to leave. The show was held in a very large park and the only way in was by car. As soon as we saw what was happening most of the English bands made a dash to get out of the park by the stage entrance before the roads got blocked. When we arrived back at the hotel we decided to hit the bar for a nightcap. We spent the night with the other groups, who bought us plenty of rounds of drinks, and naturally, the conversation was dedicated to the endless stories we all had of Lek.

Thursday June 9th was Lek's funeral at Southern Cemetery, Chorlton, Manchester. Over three hundred people turned up to pay their respects, far too many people to fit inside the chapel, so nearly two hundred listened to the service outside as it was relayed on speakers. As well as family and friends, there were many artists from the sixties and seventies music scene, including Wayne Fontana, Dave Berry, Freddie Garrity, Dave Dee, members from The Fortunes, The Swinging Blue Jeans, The Merseybeats, The Equals, Mungo Jerry, The Casuals, Marmalade, Sad Café and Graham Gouldman of 10cc. There was also a strong presence of past and present Hermits such as Geoff Foot, Graham Lee, Peter Cowap, Garth Elliot, Dave Barrow and Paul Farnell.

Our Ex-manager, Harvey Lisberg, was also present with Hal Carter, Dave Lee Travis and Mike Sweeney. If I have missed anybody out, then I apologise, as it was a very stressful day. The casket was carried into the crematorium by Karl Green, Keith Hopwood, Keith Roberts, and Rod Gerrard. There was a lovely wreath in the shape of a guitar, which I believe was sent by The Tremeloes, and Lek's hat was placed on top of the coffin. Abigail Leckenby read out a poem and I spoke about Lek's life in the band over the years. As the coffin disappeared to the tune 'There's A Kind Of Hush', an instrumental version recorded by Keith Hopwood especially for the funeral, almost everybody in the congregation was brought to tears.

At the reception after the funeral, which was held at Eltrop Grange hotel, near Manchester airport, I was chatting to Phil Kanas, our accountant. During the conversation he asked me if I was going to continue with the Herman's Hermits. I said yes and asked if there was anything I needed to do in light of the fact that I was the only original member left in the band. He told me I would have to close the partnership and bank account down immediately, and open one under the name 'Barry Whitwam Trading as Herman's Hermits'. I also had to inform HMCE/VAT, as well as all our agents, and reassure them that we would fulfil all commitments and engagements that had already been booked.

As part of the reorganisation of Herman's Hermits, I requested the Leckenby/Whitwam fax machine and computer from Leonie, so that I could begin to contact agents and the like. Leonie had decided that she wanted to manage the band now, but so intent was I on completely controlling my own destiny, I had to politely decline. I left with the fax machine and computer, but agreed to give her 10% of the income from existing bookings. I eventually managed to get hold of all of the agents that had us on their books, and got them to send duplicate contracts to me, in my name.

A few days after the contracts arrived, I telephoned Keith Hopwood to see if he would stand in again on lead guitar for Lek on the remaining shows the band had in the UK, he kindly said he would. We had a ten-week tour of the USA already booked to start at the end of June, and Keith couldn't be away that long as he had commitments with his recording studio. So, I telephoned Julie Steddom-Smith, our USA manager, and she lined us up with guitarist Paul Downing, who did an excellent job. The first engagement was at The Bayou Caddy Jubilee Casino, Lakeshore, Mississippi. We got there a day before to rehearse the songs, before starting a very enjoyable six-day run. The tour went very well and we did some return shows at the Wisconsin State Fair, International Amphitheatre, Milwaukee, and The New York State Fairgrounds, Syracuse. During this tour we had to try and organise a permanent replacement for Lek before we returned to the UK. Highly recommended was guitarist Alec Johnson, so I telephoned him from the USA and asked him if he fancied the job. He was very enthusiastic so I sent him all the songs he would have to learn by our return to the UK.

Also on this tour, I got a phone call from Diccon Hubbard who said he was arranging a show on Leonie's behalf in tribute to Lek. The gig would be at Quaffers in Stockport on the 6th September. The line-up was incredible, and included; The Four Pennies with Twinkle, The Dakotas, The Merseybeats, The Rubettes, Brian Poole & Electrix, Dave Berry & The Cruisers, Freddie & The Dreamers, The Swinging Blues Jeans, Marmalade with Dave Dee, The Tremeloes, The Troggs, Wayne Fontana & The Mind-benders with Mike Sweeney. Diccon told me that he spoken with Keith Hopwood and Karl Green, who would join Herman's Hermits for the night, along with Rod Gerrard on lead vocals and Keith Roberts on bass/vocals. He also said that we would close the show. With fourteen groups on the bill doing about thirty minutes each, that would make a total of seven hours of non-stop music. I told Diccon I wasn't having Herman's

Hermits play to an audience that were half pissed or half asleep, or an audience that had got bored and gone home, but he was insistent that we ended the night. We argued the toss about it and in the end, I told him that Herman's Hermits would go stage at ten thirty or not at all. It was settled.

The night eventually came and, sure enough, Herman's Hermits went on stage at Quaffers on 6th September at ten thirty, to a sell-out audience. We played a thirty-five-minute set, and I spoke for ten minutes about the life of my friend, Derek Leckenby. It was incredible evening with an outstanding line-up; fourteen superb bands and a fabulous audience. The only down side was the mystery of where the evening's proceeds went...

September 11th Alec Johnson played his first show as a Hermit at The Sandcastle, Blackpool, followed by several more UK shows and some dates in Denmark. Now we had a permanent line-up again, I organized a group photo shoot with Norman Taylor, who used to be one of our road crew in the sixties. I also joined the Agents Association and bought myself the agents White Book, as it was known, which had every agent in Europe listed in it. I put together a twelve-page brochure and did a mail out to at least two hundred agents. The object of the exercise was to let the world know that Herman's Hermits were still on the road, despite Lek's sad departure.

January 1995 saw us play a few shows, which was most welcome as it's usually a quiet month for groups in the UK. In February we were booked on a show called The Best Of

British, which was set to tour Australia for six weeks. Organised by Derek Franks, the bill boasted Billy J. Kramer, Brian Poole & The Electrix, The Manfreds, Gerry & The Pacemakers, and Mike Pender's Searchers. On the first night, at the Bruce Indoor Stadium in Canberra, Herman's Hermits stole the show. The next day Derek Franks came up to me and asked: "what were all those songs you played last night? I've never heard most of them."

I said we only had time for seven songs so we started with Silhouettes, which was #3 in the Australian charts, then we played A must To Avoid, a #4 hit, then Can't You Hear My Heartbeat, #3 in the charts, then Listen People. He said he'd never heard that song before. I pointed out that it made #3 in the charts in Australia.

"And what about that slow one, My Sentimental Friend, was that an album track?" I said we had to play it as it also got to #3 in the Australian charts. And, I explained, we had to do No Milk Today because it got to #1.

"That's fair enough," he said, "but why would you finish with Mrs Brown. You've Got A Lovely Daughter?"

I told him it's always best to finish your set with a #1 hit single, and explained to him that all the songs we'd played were top five hits in the Australian charts. He uttered an expletive and walked away. That night, we moved from the penultimate act of the show to top of the bill, and the audience reaction was the same, although, when Paul Jones caught up and joined the Manfreds on day four of the tour, Derek (who was the manager of the Manfreds) put them back to top of the bill.

We did some great gigs including, Sydney Entertainment Centre and Perth Entertainment Centre, both sadly closed now. After our return to the UK, we had a few shows in Germany, and then did some more shows back at home. April 6th was a sad day as we went to the funeral of a good friend of ours, Alan Barton, who was the lead singer and guitar player with Smokie. He was killed when the group's vehicle hit a hailstorm on a German autobahn. It was an accident that should never have happened, and would have been avoided if the driver hadn't been going so fast. We had travelled with said driver many times and repeatedly told him to slow down, but that would normally prompt him to speed up. In fact, he'd driven Herman's Hermits four weeks before Alan Barton was killed, and on that occasion, he nearly tipped the van over navigating a roundabout far too fast. It was all very sad.

In June, Rod Gerrard told me he wanted to quit the band. He'd fallen in love with a German girl, and like so many before, allowed it to cloud his judgement. When he came to my house and told me he was leaving, Dr Whitwam told him to think about it or go and see a psychiatrist before giving me his final answer in one week's time. He did so…went away, thought about it, but he was still leaving. I'm a believer in not wasting any time, so I telephoned Geoff Kerry, who was an ex-member of The Salford Jets, Mike Sweeney & The Thunderbirds, and Wayne Fontana & The Mindbenders. (I have actually been a Mindbender for one night when their drummer, Dave Morris (Shaky Dave), was taken seriously ill on New Year's Eve, and I stood in on drums with no rehearsal. It was a lot of fun!)

Geoff Kerry said he would love to join the band on vocals and rhythm guitar, and rehearsal started straight away. Rod Gerrard's last show was in Heide, Germany, on July 1st, then two weeks later we started a four-week tour of the USA with a new line-up.

On our return in mid-August, we had many shows in the UK, which kept us busy until mid-December, then we headed back to the States to the Jackpot Casino & Resort, Jackpot, Nevada, for a one-week engagement. The casino has always been one of our favourite places to play in the USA.

The following year we had another busy January, and as ever, incident was never far away. Towards the end of the month, after a show at Butlins in Minehead, our road manager, Micky Green, had an accident on the M5. He fell asleep at the wheel and mounted the central reservation guardrail, resulting in two wheels on either side of the barrier at sixty miles an hour. The sound of the back axle being ripped off, and the thud of the petrol tank exploding, quickly snapped him out of his sleep. The van eventually came to a stop then fell off the reservation guardrail into the fast lane of the southbound side of the M5. The police arrived soon after and were amazed that he'd walked away from the mess; there wasn't a scratch on Micky. The next day, Micky phoned me to tell me that he'd been in an accident, and that the van was a wright off. But that he was not hurt. I asked him where the van was, and he told me it was in a police compound on the M5 near Bristol. To make matters worse he had borrowed the van from a friend. Or maybe I should say ex-friend.

A day later Micky hired a van and went to pick the equipment up from the police compound. To his amazement, there wasn't anything broken, and the only casualty seemed to be a missing tom-tom leg.

Before we set off for a USA tour in the summer, there was the small matter of my 50th birthday party, which was held at Quaffers in Stockport. We billed it as A Night to Remember, and it certainly was. I invited Wayne Fontana & The Mindbenders, Dave Berry and The Cruisers, and Mike Sweeney's Explosion (and Herman's Hermits, of course) to play for the night. It was a great night but very expensive, and in hindsight, Pat and I could have gone on a world cruise for what it cost, but it was worth it.

Earlier in the year I'd been in contact with an American record producer named Doc Holiday, who had a recording studio in Hampton, Virginia. It was agreed that we would record around eight new songs that would be written by the present members of the group, and in addition we would re-record I'm Henry The Eighth and Mrs Brown, You've Got A Lovely Daughter. The CD was going to be called That Was Then, This Is Now, and it was agreed that all four members of the band would share the writing and publishing equally, regardless of input. I have had some bad experiences over the years regarding the distribution of writing credits, so splitting everything four ways would be the simplest and fairest thing to do. Oh boy, was I wrong.

We left Manchester on the 16th July to start our tour of the USA, as part of which I had organised the trip to Hampton to record the new CD. I had booked a nice hotel close to the recording studio (at my own expense) and we had eight strong songs ready to record. When we finally got to Hampton to start recording, it turned out that the studio was all new, and Doc Holiday was still learning how to use it properly, so it took a lot longer than expected to get the tracks recorded. In the end, Doc Holiday was very pleased with tracks, but he said he needed one more song to finish the CD. Keith said he had a song that could be added, so he played it to us all on an acoustic guitar, and we all liked it. Keith and I laid down the drum and bass tracks, then Geoff Kerry and Alec Johnson put their guitars on. The vocals were added and the song sounded just as good as the rest of the songs we'd recorded.

After a few listens of the track, Doc Holiday said this song would be perfect for Steven Seagal's new film, which Doc was producing the soundtrack for. I heard Keith say: "that's more money for Keithy". I asked him what he meant by that, but he just brushed it off. When we got back to the hotel I went to his room and asked him again what he meant by saying "more money for Keithy". He said that the last song, which was going to be used in Steven Seagal's next film, was his and not part of the four ways split. I reminded him that we had an agreement, and that the song was recorded for the CD, all of which would be divided equally between the four members of the group. I have never seen a person change so much in a few minutes.

Over the rest of the tour, Keith tried to make a separate deal with me regarding the song and the CD. I said no, and that we had a deal with Geoff Kerry and Alec Johnson. At Chicago airport while waiting in the departure lounge for our plane home to Manchester, I informed everyone that I had instructed a lawyer to set up a publishing company and contract between us for all the songs we had recorded for Doc Holiday. We had one week off before we departed for a tour of Australia, and I was frankly glad to get away from Keith.

A week soon passed and before we knew it, we were in a jumbo jet hurtling down the runway at Manchester Airport. Just before the plane left the ground, Keith, who was sat across the aisle from me, said he could be at home writing hit records rather than doing this shit. I pretended that I had not heard him, although I could have happily punched him in the face at that moment. I reminded myself that it's not a good idea to start a fight on an aircraft. Two weeks into the tour I received a package from the lawyer with the details of the publishing company and contract regarding the new CD. I had four photocopies made and gave a copy to each of the boys in the band, and told them to read through it and we would sign it tomorrow if they all agreed. The next morning there was a knock on my hotel room. It was Keith, smelling like a brewery. He said he wasn't signing anything and not giving 'the other two fuckers' a penny of his money. I thought 'that's a funny way to hand in your resignation'. I asked if that was his last word on the matter, to which he replied "yes".

I checked on the time different to UK and made a telephone call to Geoff Foot to see if he would like his old job back as frontman and bass guitarist. He said he was working with Wayne Fontana at the moment, but would love to come back to Herman's Hermits. And so it was…the day after we got back to the UK we had a show down south in a big hotel, and this (little did he know it) would be Keith Roberts' last show.

After the show I arranged with the other three to meet at Keith's house on the Monday morning for a meeting. At 11.00am on that Monday, Geoff Kerry, Alec Johnson and I arrived at Keith's house. We sat in his front room and I said that I wanted Geoff and Alec to hear what he'd said to me in Australia about them. In the end I had to recount the conversation and explain to Geoff and Alec what he'd said about them. With that, I said the three of us would continue working as Herman's Hermits with Geoff Foot, and that he, Keith, was fired. We left him standing in his front room, white with shock.

Two days later we were rehearsing with Geoff Foot. Although it had been five years since Geoff left the band, he fell straight back into the songs and as a result the band sounded a hundred percent better. I read in the newspaper six months later that Steven Seagal had been presented with lots of songs for his latest film and had thought they were all rubbish, so was writing his own songs for the film. I telephoned Doc Holiday a week after Geoff Foot had re-joined the band and told him that Keith Roberts had left the band, and that the art work would have to be changed. He wasn't pleased as he'd pressed 15,000 copies. We fell out and the CD was shelved.

In 1997 we did four tours of the USA, organised by Julie Steddom Smith, our American manager. The first was just a short visit in February playing for a week in Cactus Pete's Resort Casino in Jackpot, Nevada, then onto Mohegan Casino, Uncasville, Connecticut, before heading home to play some UK shows. We had a sixteen-day tour of Germany and on our return, we were booked on Queen Elizabeth 2 for a three-week cruise of the Mediterranean, visiting Italy, Sicily, Corfu, Turkey, Greece, Sardinia and Majorca, and for the first time the QE 2 went to Istanbul. We all took our wives with us and had a fabulous time. I remember walking round the Bazaar in Istanbul with Geoff Foot and I bought a leather rider's cap, and I wore it all the way back to the meeting place where we met up with the girls. Pat took one look at my new cap and said: "and where do think you're going to wear that? You look like Rudolf Nureyev". I have never worn the cap since.

The great thing about cruises is that you only do one show a week, so we performed just three shows in 21 days for the passengers, and one for the crew in their own club, called The Pig & Whistle. We had a great night playing for the crew; we started playing at midnight and finished at five in the morning. A few of the crew were musicians so they stood in so we could have some rests. The beer was endless… crate after crate were placed in front of the stage, and we did our best to make sure none was left by the time we finished playing. We made some great friends on the cruise including Jim Bowen, (who was telling jokes in the Golden Lion Pub); Peter Sissons (an English journalist and broadcaster); Stewart Bates (a Concorde Pilot who gave some talks about the making of and flying of Concorde); and Peter Dean (who we nicknamed Dr Death because he was a coroner who gave lectures on Jack the Ripper).

At the end of the day, we would all meet up and tell jokes and stories about being in the entertainment business. It was a fabulous cruise and we went on to do three more cruises, two of which were across the Atlantic. On our return to the UK we had a week off and I was having lunch with Pat and Frank, her father, when I got a phone call from Peter Noone. After a few pleasantries he asked me if I would like to join him on stage at the London Palladium along with Karl Green and Keith Hopwood. I said I would love to and asked what time the show started knowing that Pat and I could just about make it in time if we left Manchester then.

The show was just like old times. I didn't realise at the time, but it had been twenty-six years since the four of us had been on the same stage together. At the end of the show, we had a sandwich and a beer then a photo was taken of the four of us with Peter's father Dennis. Pat and I drove home after the show kind of shell shocked and tired. It had been a long day.

Mid-tour in August of 1997, the Wisconsin lottery jackpot had reached over eighty million dollars, so I told everyone in the band that they really should buy tickets for that Saturday night's draw, so we all headed to a local gas station in Thiensville on Friday afternoon to try our luck. We had a show on the Saturday night, so we couldn't check the results until Sunday morning. We were all sat around a large table filling ourselves with breakfast and coffee on the Sunday morning, all apart from Alec Johnson, our then guitarist. I had already checked the lottery results, and we'd had no winners.

Just then, Alec appeared and went into the bathroom, and a plan quickly hatched in my mind. I went into his room, opened his wallet and found the ten lottery tickets he'd bought. I quickly copied the numbers from one of his tickets and was back at the table before he'd come out of the bathroom.

Ten minutes later he was at the table having a piece of toast and a cup of tea, when I mentioned that we'd had already checked our tickets and sadly won nothing. He went to his bedroom and got his wallet and came back with his tickets. I had written his numbers on the same page as the lottery results. I read out two rows of numbers from the newspaper, before starting to read out his numbers. After I read out his first three numbers, he started to get really excited, then I quickly read the final numbers and the two bonus numbers. Alec went crazy shouting that he'd won the lottery. By virtue of the fact that I was hiding behind the newspaper and my hands were shaking with laughter, it didn't take him long to realize he'd been set up. Well, at least he thought he was a millionaire for a few seconds.

A cruise to New York sounds, and is, rather glamorous, but one inescapable fact is that you spend six days crossing the Atlantic, so you have to find things to do. One of the cruises this year moved on to Boston and Halifax after New York. Because of Cunard's generosity regarding accommodation on board, I invited Dave and Eileen Evans as our road crew for the trip; there wasn't much to carry but, like the rest of us, they got a double cabin. As we were boarding the ship in

Southampton, Geoff Kerry had mentioned to me that he had bought a thousand pounds worth of shares in Newcastle United Football club. I thought nothing more about it until we were three days into crossing the Atlantic. The weather was vile and you couldn't go on deck, so I met Dave in The Red Lion pub for a pint or two and a chat. During the conversation I told Dave about Geoff Kerry buying a thousand pound of shares in Newcastle United, and we came up with devious idea. The QE2 had a daily newspaper (which was printed on-board) with UK and world headlines, along with various items of cruise information. We went to the ship's pressroom and had a little chat with the person in charge of printing the ship's newspaper. He gave us permission to print one special copy that had been tailored to our needs.

The next day we kept a look out for Geoff and eventually found him in the shop. I went up to him, handed him the newspaper, and told him there was something about Newcastle United. Dave and I snuck off and hid behind a clothing rack as he read the article, which turned him white as a sheet. The false article stated that Newcastle United had gone bankrupt, and that the value of shares had been wiped out overnight. The passengers who saw Dave and I crouching behind the clothes rack laughing our heads off, must have thought we'd gone mad. We gave Geoff ten minutes to get over the shock of losing one thousand pounds before we told him it was a joke and that we had put the article in his newspaper. I don't think he saw the funny side but acknowledged the time and effort that had been expended in setting up the gag.

Back at home and it was straight back to reality with a sixties weekend at Butlins in Pwllheli, Wales, a venue which would close a year later. There was still just enough time for a quick one-month tour of Australia before Christmas.

We finally arrived home on the 17th of December. The day before we flew home, I was body surfing at Manly Beach in Sydney, so arrived home with a great sun tan to a house decorated for Christmas. As well as managing to complete four tours of the USA, two cruises on the QE2 and a tour of Australia, it had been a pretty good year.

In 1998 we did three tours of the USA, the first of which ran from late January until March. Cactus Pete's Resort Casino in Jackpot, Nevada, was one of our favourite venues and always a joy to go back to. Jackpot is only a quarter of a mile from the northern edge of Nevada, so the little town is a very popular gambling destination with the residents of nearby Idaho. Jackpot has a population of just over a thousand people, and most of them work at the casino. After Cactus Pete's we had a week touring Montana playing at Billing, Helena, and Butte. I must say that Montana really is a fabulous place to visit, and the scenery is amazing.

On our return to the UK, we set off immediately to Germany once again, mainly playing in Troisdorf, Dresden, Gera, Chemnitz and Leipzig, places we visited every time we toured there. May saw us traveling to Skien in Norway with our old mates The Swinging Blue Jeans, Mungo Jerry, and Showaddywaddy, to do a TV show called The Golden Hits. A few more shows in Germany and Austria, and we were on our way back to the USA.

While we were in the Wisconsin area, we stayed at Bobbi Britten's house, in Thiensville. Bobbi was a good friend and it was good to spend some time in her house rather than a hotel room. The next village to Thiensville was called Mequon where another good friend of ours, Paul Edwards, had a recording studio called Rainbow Studios. We recorded a CD-Single called Songs of Yesterday (written by Harrison/Schmidt/Altenbrockster), which was to be released in Germany on the Megaphone label. When we had finished the recording we sent the track to Jeff Harrison in Germany, who, thanks to some production wizardry, improved the track 100%. I honestly think the song should have been a hit, but Megaphone was a small company with limited financial resources and as result the song didn't trouble any charts.

In January of 1999 we were booked to do three shows in Norway with Gerry and the Pacemakers, and Freddie and the Dreamers. We landed in Oslo and took a connecting flight to Trondheim, which was where our first show was. The weather was atrocious, and there was heavy snow and a thick mist; it looked like we wouldn't make this connection. There was an announcement over the PA system that all incoming flights were cancelled and only departures were permitted. When it was time to board the plane I became a little apprehensive...I have seen conditions half as bad as this at Manchester airport, and the airport would be closed until the weather was clear. All I could keep telling myself as I fastened my safety belt is that the pilot wouldn't fly the plane if it was dangerous. As it turned out, the plane took off without any problems and we soon broke through the clouds into lovely blue sky...all our troubles were over. It was only a small plane with seats for about forty passengers, and the flight to Trondheim was due to take around one and a half hours. One hour and twenty minutes later the captain made an announcement to say that Trondheim airport had just closed due to the fact it had been snowed under and no planes could land. The captain informed us that we were going to Bergen, which was now the only airport open. The tour promoter made a phone call to the venue in Trondheim and told them that we could not land there, so they should cancel the show and the transport arrangements from the airport to our hotel. Most of the people on the flight were involved in the tour.

Forty minutes later the captain came into the main cabin with a grim expression on his face and said that Bergen airport had just informed him that that airport was closed as well. He also told us that we couldn't stay in the air all day and that we would have to try and land somewhere soon, as we only had enough fuel left for about one hour, at the most. We all agreed. Somebody shouted out that if we were going to crash, let's crash in Trondheim where the show was going to be...if we make the landing, then we can do the show, and if we die, then we died trying. The captain went back into the cockpit and turned the plane around. You could have heard a pin drop...nobody said a word as we all wondered if it would be our last flight. I considered the headlines...3 Sixties Groups Perish in Norwegian Snowstorm!

The captain made another announcement after about thirty minutes saying that he'd radioed Trondheim airport to tell the tower that we were going to land one way or another. Apparently, the authorities at the airport had told the pilot that they would plough as much of the runway as they could in the time they had, and wished him good luck. I took out a Clive Cussler book from my bag – I had one chapter left to read, it would be nice to finish it before we landed or crashed. Just as I finished the last page I looked out of the window and saw snow on the ground, a matter of feet below. As the wheels touched the ground and the engines went into reverse thrust, and the plane started to decelerate. There was a thunderous sound of cheering from everybody on board…we had made it. The promoter rang the venue up to tell them that the tour had landed at Trondheim airport and to get the transport back to pick us up and put the show back on. The show was a great success; the venue had told the radio station and local TV to make an announcement that the show was going ahead as planned.

The next day the tour flew back to Oslo for a concert at the Oslo Konserthus. The airport had been cleared of snow overnight so there was no problem landing now. The last show of the three-day tour was in Stavanger and then back home to a well-deserved rest before heading off to the USA and Canada for a three-week tour.

I remember staying in a hotel in downtown Winnipeg in the middle of February; by God it was cold…at least minus twenty centigrade. We had a night off so the band decided to go to the pub across the road for some R & R. Now Winnipeg town centre has lots of walkways connecting the shops and malls so you don't have to go outside in the freezing cold to get to the other side of the road. The pub was no more than a hundred yards away across the road, so we decided it would be quicker to walk across the road rather than take a walkway. We left the hotel with some briskness, and walked into a wind chill of about fifty below. Within seconds the brisk walk had turned into a mad gallop. It took just thirty seconds to get to the pub, but in that short time my whole body had gone numb and my face felt like it was about to crack and fall of. After a few minutes of warning up I ordered four pints of Canadian Moose Head beer. We played pool for about two hours and the beer was flowing nicely. Later, I ordered another round. I took the pints over to lads by the pool table and went back to pay for them, but the bar tender said that would be thirty dollars for the five drinks. I said we have only had four pints, which should be twenty-five dollars, but he said I had ordered five pints this time and that it would be thirty dollars.

I was just about to start arguing with him when he said: "pay up or get out". Seeing as it was cold enough to freeze off extremities within seconds outside, I said "no problem", and walked back to the pool table. I told the lads that the barman had ripped me off for five dollars, to which Geoff Foot said he would sort him out, even though I said he'd throw us out if we started anything. We eventually finished our pints and ran back across the road to the hotel…funny, it didn't seem as cold with five pints of beer inside us. Geoff was still going on about the bent barman. I said: "forget it, I got you a souvenir to remember our night in a Winnipeg bar," and handed over the eight ball which I pinched on the way out. That must have been worth about five dollars.

After the USA/Canadian tour we had a week off before we went to Japan for a week at the Sweet Basil, Tokyo. I was pretty excited as the last time I was there was in 1966. Prior to the trip, a TV station had been in touch to arrange a video of the show, which meant we could put out a CD called Live In Japan. On the night of the recording, Geoff Kerry, our rhythm guitarist and vocalist introduced the band and said hello to the audience in Japanese. I had forgotten that Geoff Kerry's sister had married a Japanese man years before and could speak the language fluently. I was suitably impressed, as was the audience who gave him a tremendous round of applause. As the applause was dying down, and not realising that my microphone was live, I said: "Geoff Kerry has just ordered meat pie and chips, mushy pies with gravy four times". As it happens, the video turned out fabulously and can be found on YouTube, and is entitled 'Herman's Hermits Live In Japan'.

On our return to the UK, we had a week off and then moved on to the Duarte Gardens, Casino Estoril, Portugal. The show went very, and we also made good friends with the promoter (we only remembered his name as Carlos) who, nine months later booked us again…but more on that later.

On our return to the UK, we did the usual round of shows. On 1st June we did a charity show for Colin Manley, who was the lead guitarist with The Swinging Blue Jeans until he died of cancer in April of that year. Colin was one of the nicest guys you could ever meet, and it was a pleasure to be on the show. On the show with us were The Searchers, The Merseybeats, The Remo & Friends, Vince Earl and Band, The Story Book Show featuring Marmalade, Dave Dee & Chip Hawkes, Ray Brown, and Peter Sarstedt. A CD and video of the concert was released by Pilar (UK) Ltd in 2000.

July and August saw another tour of the USA covering Nevada, Arizona, Mississippi, Wisconsin and Iowa. The highlight of the tour was playing at the Oshkosh, Wisconsin EAA air show. This show is held every year and there are hundreds of planes filling the sky all day long. On our return to the UK, I started to get lots of phone call from other groups asking me what they should charge for a show on New Year's Eve, being the Millennium. I said I had no idea, but one of the guys in the band said that local groups were charging up to two thousand pounds a show. Then pubs started charging fifty pounds just to go into a pub for a drink, never mind a meal. It was at this time I got a telephone call from our friend Carlos at the Casino Estoril in Lisbon offering the band a gig on New Year's Eve. Without giving it much thought I told him the fee would be six times what he paid us the last time, plus twelve air tickets. He said no problem and also said James Brown would be on the bill the same night. It was a brilliant night and we got to spend some time with James Brown as well. He was nice to talk to, put on an incredible show (as you'd expect), and his band was fantastic. At twelve o'clock there was a firework display which went on for half an hour... God knows what the tickets cost to get into the show that night; it must have been a small fortune. The champagne was free and flowing all-night and by the time Pat and I got to bed it was gone four in the morning.

The next day we had a day off so we all went for a walk along the promenade. It was cold and the sea was blowing up a storm, so Pat and I decided to go into Lisbon to do some shopping. Altogether we had three days in Portugal, and got handsomely paid for it.

11

A New Millennium

One of the very first things we did in the new millennium was to appear on This Is Your Life (hosted by Michael Aspel) to help honour the career of legendary DJ Dave Lee Travis. All of the surviving members of Herman's Hermits made it onto the show, although Peter appeared courtesy of a recorded message. As I mentioned earlier in this book, Dave Lee Travis was our tour manager and warm-up act for one tour of the States in 1965. He was already a successful DJ in the UK at the time, but wanted to expand his horizons. I have to say he was much better as a DJ than a tour manger. On the tour he went for an audition at a radio station and apparently did very well, but didn't get the job because he didn't have the required licence to use the electrical equipment in the studios. It was a great shame because I'm sure Dave would have made a great career in the USA, what with his thick Mancunian accent.

In February we started a tour of the USA and Canada. We began, once again, at Cactus Pete's, Jackpot, Nevada, which being a thousand feet above sea level, was just about as cold as one could bear. We then moved on to Arizona Charlie's in Las Vegas, and then on to the relative warmth of the Hon-Dah Casino in Pinetop, Arizona, for a one-week engage-ment. I had been having trouble with my microphone for three nights…it was randomly going off and on, every time I spoke through it, and after every show I would ask the in-house sound engineer to fix it or replace it with a new one. During the fourth night, the microphone was even worse (I sounded like Norman Collier), so I announced through the ailing microphone that I was going to stick the mic up his ass when the show was over. The funny thing was though, that the microphone was as clear as a bell when I said that…of course. I don't think the soundman had much of a sense of humour though, as we never appeared at the casino ever again.

If we thought Jackpot was cold, we then flew off for a two-day engagement at McPhillips Street Station, Winnipeg, which is a casino open twenty-three hours a day. They have one hour between five and six o'clock in the morning to empty the machines and spruce the place up, and of course this is the only time the bands can sound check. So, it's a very bleary-eyed set up and check, then to the hotel and back to bed.

After returning back to the UK Geoff Kerry announced he was tired of being on the road for three quarters of the year, and wanted a quieter life with his girlfriend, Lynne. Geoff's last show was in Torquay, then on the 15th April he was replaced by Graham Caunce, a.k.a Graham Lee, nicknamed Monty. Monty was the perfect man for the job as he had already done a three-week tour of Sweden with us when he stood in for Lek in 1992 (whilst he was undergoing chemotherapy). Monty played guitar similar to Lek, so Alec Johnson and Monty could share the lead parts. Monty had already had some success with his band The Scorpions (not to be confused with the German rock outfit of the same name), and in Manchester with The Chancellors and The Pressmen. The rest of the year was very busy with lots of shows in the UK as well as trips to the USA and Canada, Australia, Finland, Sweden and New Year's Eve in Germany.

We began the following year in familiar fashion by jetting off for an engagement at Cactus Pete's in Jackpot, Nevada, recording the show for a new CD while we were there. It was only a three-week stint, then straight back to the UK for a number of shows before we set off on a tour of Australia and New Zealand in the spring. On our return we were back to Germany and Denmark before going on yet another tour of the USA and Canada. While we were at the Club Regent Casino in Winnipeg, the in-house soundman recorded the show, which was supposed to be sent on to us after remixing it. We never received it but were told later that it was released on the Moonraker/Hyacinth record label. Let's hope it was good!

At the end of July, we flew to Hawaii to join a six-day cruise around the islands. As we were waiting to board the ship, five old guys were coming down the gangplank carrying a couple of guitars and a snare drum. We asked them what band they were in and one of them said they were Bill Haley's Comets – apparently, they had two original members still in the group. What a thrill to meet a couple of members of one of the iconic rock and roll bands of the fifties. When we finally got on board we were greeted by the cruise director, and after introductions he said he hoped we were more livelily than the last group!

For six days we had the ship rocking and rolling. While passing an active volcano in the dark the captain made an announcement to say if anybody wants to see it then they should go to the port side of the ship. Of course, everybody was on the deck looking apart from Geoff Foot and myself. I said to Geoff: "when you've seen one volcano in the dark, you've seen them all," so we had another drink at the bar.

On our return to the UK Alec Johnson left the band, and was replaced by keyboard player Gary Powell. Since 1999, Peter Noone had been using the billing of 'Herman's Hermits Starring Peter Noone' in America, and what had been a very lucrative market controlled by Whitwam/Leckenby since the early 70s had now been split between two competing versions of Herman's Hermits. So, when Alec left, my original thought was to get Karl Green to re-join the band. To have two original members in the line-up would obviously be an advantage in the competition with Peter Noone for USA bookings. Sadly though, 2001 was a very difficult year for Karl Green for various personal reasons, so a comeback with Herman's Hermits would have to wait. Gary Powell was probably a bit too young for the band, but finding musicians who can be away from home for long periods of time are few and far between. Gary's first show was at The Civic Centre in Chelmsford on September 5th.

The September 11th terror attack on the World Trade Centre sent a shockwave around the world and had ramifications on the international live entertainment industry, especially in and out of the United States. We'd done our last scheduled trip to the States for the year, so saw out the remainder of 2001 busily visiting every corner of the UK and Europe.

In February of 2002 we returned to Cactus Pete's for a week, and during that time I realised that Gary Powell was far too young looking to be in the band, and that I would have to start looking for a more suitable, 'vintage' keyboard player.

In March we did a big show in Berlin with The Animals and a variety of other groups. We went down a storm and came off to a standing ovation. The promoter, Rudi Hauptman, who was standing in the wings, told us to go back and do another song. I said I preferred to leave the audience wanting more, but he was insistent that we did one more song. We enthusiastically ran back out and started to play Jeff Beck's Hi Ho Silver Lining, assuming that it would bring the house down. How wrong we were. We finished the song and came off stage to the sound of our own boots; the promoter said he'd never heard the song before, and it was clear that the audience shared that sentiment. To coin an old expression…one minute you're up the next minute you're down.

Back in Manchester a few days later I had a meeting with Gary and told him that unfortunately he was being replaced because he was too young for the band. It's a rotten job telling people they are no longer in the band, but it just wasn't working. Gary's replacement was Robert Birrell (born November 1948), a Scotsman who'd been living in Manchester for about thirty years. Robert had been playing keyboards since the 60's and toured with many bands in the UK and abroad over the years. Nine months earlier his old mate Graham Lee (Monty) had tried to recruit him for Herman's Hermits, an offer he then declined, but regretted. When asked again Robert jumped at the chance of playing and touring with us.

One night after a show, Robert told me a story that still makes me laugh to this day. He was once a television repairman and he recounted the occasion one cold winter's day when he had to go and fix a broken TV. An old lady showed him to the front room, where the ailing TV sat in the corner of the room. He had to push an armchair off the way in order to get to the TV, but didn't realise that he'd pushed it right up to a blazing electric fire. After a few minutes he got the TV working and came out from behind it to see the armchair fully on fire. The old lady came into the room, saw the scene, and got a bucket of water, which she threw over the armchair. She screamed at Robert to get out of her house, which he quickly did. By the time Robert had got back to the repair shop, the old lady had phoned his boss and he was fired on the spot…no pun intended.

July and August saw us on another tour of the USA, organised by our stateside manager Julie Steddom-Smith. However, on this occasion I was forced to stop advertising American shows on my website as some of Peter Noone's fans

(Noonatics, as some people called them) kept on pestering club owners and promoters with emails and phone calls, in an attempt to stop them booking what they liked to call 'The Hermanless Hermits'.

On August 26th Peter Noone filed a lawsuit in the Los Angeles District Court, against me and the other members of my band, as well as my USA agents. The lawsuit stated that 'Whitwam was an unskilled drummer and not involved in most of the group's hits', and also claims that 'the group led by Whitwam is an inferior entertainment product lacking any true connection with Herman's Hermits'. Noone's lawsuit sought an injunction blocking myself and the other three band members from performing as Herman's Hermits in the USA. Even though Peter left Herman's Hermits some thirty years before, and the entire allegation made by him was completely groundless, the legal battle between the lawyers representing both sides would last for the next ten months. The problem with USA justice system is if somebody files against you, you have to answer the lawsuit in twenty-eight days or you lose the case and have to pay the other side's costs. Peter Noone and Kennedy Street Artists Ltd had already tried to stop Karl Green, Derek Leckenby and myself from using the name Herman's Hermits in August 1975. It went to the High Court of Justice, Queen's Bench Division, where we won the right to call our band 'Herman's Hermits', and also prohibited Peter Noone and his agents from using the word 'Hermits' in conjunction with the word 'Herman' or 'Herman's'.

When Peter signed up with Paradise Artists in the USA, they obviously put two fingers up to the court order and started to book Peter out as 'Herman's Hermits Starring Peter Noone'. In 2003, it was finally agreed by Peter Noone and myself that when I worked in the USA, I would call my group 'Herman's Hermits Starring Barry Whitwam', and he could call himself 'Herman's Hermits Starring Peter Noone'. This agreement was only for the USA, however. For the rest of the world, I was still entitled to call my group 'Herman's Hermits'. This was a total waste of a lot of money on both sides, and could have been agreed on the phone, but Peter got lawyered-up and it was obvious that he wanted to stop me from touring the USA, period. When we got back to the UK we spent the rest of the year touring Denmark, Germany, Norway as well as lot of shows in England.

2003 was another busy year, in spite of it being the first time since Herman's Hermits were born that we hadn't toured America. That aside, the first chunk of the year was spent all over the UK, and various parts of Europe.

On the 30th May, Mickie Most died. This was a very sad time for me. Apart from being Herman's Hermits recording producer from 1964 to 1971, he also produced The Animals, Lulu, Donovan, Nashville Teens, Jeff Beck, The Yardbirds, Hot Chocolate, Suzi Quatro, Cozy Powell, Racey, Kim Wilde and many others. Mickie died of peritoneal mesothelioma; a rare form of cancer associated with exposure to asbestos. Mickie's funeral was on June 9th, and Peter Noone was there with what looked like a six-foot six bodyguard. Maybe he thought I was going plant one on him for all the trouble he caused with his stupid lawsuits.

June 17th saw us set off for a tour of Australia for five weeks. We returned to a string of dates in the UK and Norway, and then at the end of September we toured Denmark, Austria and Holland with The Tremeloes and The Swinging Blue Jeans. November 1st was by far the most memorable evening of the year. We were booked for a performance at the Convention Centre in Harrogate, for the Lady's Barbershop Association, with five hundred excitable ladies in attendance. The highlight of the show was at the end of Something Is Happening, where we usually get everybody to sing – 'the same thing, same thing, same thing, is happening to me', on their own, before I bring the band back in. I couldn't bring the song back in as five hundred ladies sang 'the same thing, same thing, same thing' in a five-hundred-part harmony, and laughter prevented me from continuing. Geoff would usually tell the audience they were terrible, and get them to try again until they got it right…but not this night. He told them they were brilliant, just so we could get to the end of the song.

From mid-November until Christmas, we were kept busy on the road with P.J. Proby, The Troggs, Mike Pender's Searchers and The Ivy League on The Sixties Gold 40th Anniversary Tour. During one of the sound checks (which we did straight after PJ Proby's) I sat behind the drums a bit too quickly before the monitor man had had time to change the monitor mix. PJ's drummer, Peter Thomas, wore headphones as he had the Proby backing tracks in his headphones, as a result the monitor had the drum mix at a ridiculous volume. I sat down and did a drum roll around the kit, which nearly knocked me off my stool. When the ringing in my ears finally stopped, we did the sound check. Half an hour before show time I had an odd episode when the dressing room spun for a moment or two. Ten minutes before the show I went down to see John Craig, our tour manager, and by this time the room was properly spinning and I was violently sick. I bounced off every wall into his office. He took one look at me and rang for an ambulance. As I lay on the couch in his office the ceiling was spinning even faster. In those few minutes waiting for the ambulance to arrive John Craig had prepared Peter Thomas to learn the Herman's Hermits set, as I was going straight to Dorchester hospital.

I would like to thank the ambulance crew who did a fantastic job getting from Weymouth to Dorchester in ten minutes with the blue lights and siren on all the way. Mike Pender of the Searchers had seen me being taken into an ambulance and assumed I'd had a heart attack, and very quickly, with help from the internet, the news that I had indeed had one was most of the way around the world.

In the ambulance, the medics wired me up to a monitor that transmitted all my vital signs to the hospital in preparation for my arrival. Everything was still spinning and I'd never felt so sick in my life, and I wondered if this was what it felt like to have a heart attack. Soon enough, I was with a doctor, and having looked at my vital signs, he assured me that everything was normal and that I hadn't had a heart attack. He asked me if I had been drinking alcohol…not a drop, I replied. He asked me if anything unusual had happened in the last few hours or so. I told him about the loud sound check, to which he smiled and told me I'd had a severe attack of vertigo. He prescribed some pills for me to last until I got home and saw my own doctor, which was three days later. After a bit of rest and observation in the hospital, the lads picked me up and we all got back to the hotel in Weymouth, where I was immediately sick again.

The next day was a day off and I was feeling much better with no dizziness, so that night we went to the pub and had a curry. The next day, after our sound check, I was feeling rough again and felt dizzy so I lay down under a table in the dressing room. John Craig came in to ask how I was…I said I was still a bit dizzy, but I should be okay for the show in two hours. John put scaffolding around the drum riser in case I fell backwards off the rostrum, but I didn't and the show went very well. We went home the next day and my doctor prescribed some tablets that would help with the dizziness. It only ever happened twice after that; once sat on the sofa watching the TV with Pat, and the other time – more terrifyingly – whilst driving on the M56 motorway. Thankfully, it only lasted a few seconds. It turns out that many musicians get vertigo due to the volumes on stage. It was an eventful episode but it was a great tour as we were all good friends.

In April 2004 Graham Lee, decided that the traveling was getting too much for him, and that it was time to leave the band. He was replaced by Eddy Carter who'd started his musical career in a band called Flashback, and boasted an appearance on New Faces, and in the 90s he was with Steve

Wright's Easybeats. In May we headed off to Australia, with one show in Singapore on the way. The tour was organised by Richard Brown, our Australia agent at the time. The tour kicked off in Perth, Western Australia, in a venue called The Breakwater, which is a lot better than it sounds. It was right on the coast near Freemantle…the atmosphere was fantastic and the Barramundi fish dinner Ken Reed (the owner) provided for us was out of this world. After Freemantle we travelled south by road, working our way down to Esperance on the southern coast of Australia then travelled back north to Perth for one show. We then hit, Newman, Karratha and ten other towns before we arrived in Broome. Esperance to Broome, via all the towns we played, is about 4000km, and we travelled in a big coach that had air conditioning, but typically it didn't work. Some of the trips were made through the night just to avoid the heat of the day. The problem is that night-time is when kangaroos like to play chicken with unsuspecting vehicles on Australia's roads. There were many casualties.

The petrol stations and rest areas were often 350km apart. The toilets were like wooden shacks and, on one occasion when concluding my relief, I pulled the chain and a giant frog slid out from under the rim and stuck itself to the inside of the toilet bowl. It was probably the only available water in several kilometres. After Western Australia we flew to Queensland. We went to Brisbane stopping off for shows in Caloundra, Hervey Bay, Bundaberg, Rockhampton, Mackay, Proserpine, Townsville, and finished the tour in Cairns on the 28th June, before flying back to the UK.

On 22nd July we headed to the States (after last year's interlude) for another four-week tour organised by Julie Steddom-Smith. On this visit I experienced one of the most stressful days of my life. We had a show at the Lac Courte Oreilles Casino in Hayward, Wisconsin, and the next day we had to drive to Minneapolis to catch a mid-day flight to Boston. We set off in plenty of time but got hopelessly lost on the way to the airport. What was supposed to be a two-hour drive had turned into three and half hours, and we were still miles from the airport. At one point I looked out of the car window and saw a plane with its landing gear down, so I told the driver to follow the plane. We got to the kerb-side check-in with twenty-five minutes to spare before the plane was due to take off. The airport check-in guy said to get the guitars and baggage on his trolley as the gate was closing in two minutes. I gave him a fifty-dollar bill and he assured me that he'd make sure the baggage got on the plane. With tickets in hand, we all ran to security with about ten minutes before the gate was to close. The bags went slowly through the x-ray machine, then, just as my bag went in, a red light pinged on.

The Security officer asked whose bag it was. I raised my hand and he told me to open it. I explain that I only have five minutes to get on board my plane, but he explained that wasn't his problem. Geoff Foot made it to the departure gate first and warned the flight attendant that there were three more people coming right behind him. She looked but saw nobody. Geoff kept her talking as one by one the lads got to the door of the aircraft, and went on board. In the end, Geoff stood in the way as she tried to close the door, but I arrived just in time and squeezed through the remaining gap in the door, and got myself aboard. She slammed the door shut and announced that everybody was aboard as the plane pushed back.

The show in Falmouth was at 7.00pm in an open-air park and was only 80 miles from Boston airport. So, with a three-hour, fifteen-hundred-mile flight and a one-hour time zone change, we were due to arrive in Boston at 4.00pm. We had to wait half an hour for the guitars and baggage to arrive at the carousel, and when they did, we were one guitar short. While baggage handlers were trying to find the guitar, I went to car hire to pick up a people carrier, and by the time I got back to arrivals, the boys were waiting outside for me on the kerb… still one guitar down. The lads had told the airline to hold onto the guitar until the next day as we were flying back to Milwaukee and could pick it up then. Now we have two hours to travel 80 miles to Falmouth. No problem.

But then, heading south on interstate 93 I make a huge mistake; instead of staying on the 93 south and then picking up highway 24 south to Interstate 495, I instead turned off and got on highway 3A, and all of a sudden, we were driving through the suburbs of Boston heading towards the east coast road. We made a quick stop to telephone Julie, our manager in California, and asked her to call the promoter in Falmouth and get us a six-string guitar, oh yes, and to tell him we may be late getting there.

Somehow, at 6.45pm, with fifteen minutes to spare, we roll through the gates of the park and go straight to the stage. The crew were setting the stage for us, as per our stage plan that had been sent to them a week before, and one of the stagehands handed us a guitar, which had even been tuned. We did a quick monitor check and started the show exactly at 7.00pm. The show was a great success and afterwards we checked into our hotel for a well-earned few pints of beer, which just about calmed my nerves.

In October, and a little less stressful, we played a P&O cruise with The Fortunes on the Adonia, travelling from Southampton to Spain and back, all in seven days. The cruise, which was stuffed full of sixties music fans, was compered by Ed 'Stewpot' Stewart. One evening Ed interviewed us for an hour in front of five hundred passengers in the concert lounge…it was a lot of fun. The year was wrapped up back on another 60s Gold 40th Anniversary Tour of the UK, sharing the bill with PJ Proby, The Troggs, and The Ivy League.

We had some disappointment at the beginning of 2005 when a Russian tour, scheduled for April, was cancelled because the Russians wouldn't let us take the fee out of the country. At the end of April, we do manage to get to Australia for a five-week tour. But then, on our return, we should have flown straight to India for a short tour, but that was cancelled because of threats of terrorism. Then in July…if you can believe it, a two-week tour of Japan, Oman, the United Arab Emirates and Saudi Arabia was pulled, as the promoter was worried about terrorism in the Middle East leg.

In spite of these obstacles, we had a very busy year, which included a ten-day tour of Denmark (sometimes billing with The Animals and The Fortunes) followed by a lengthy tour of

Sweden (The Golden Sixties Tour) accompanied by The Tremeloes and The Swinging Blue Jeans. In November we released a single called When The Children Start Laughing. It was a lovely song but didn't make the charts. We were supposed to play New Year's Eve in Washington D.C., but, quite fittingly, it was cancelled.

January 2006 kicked off with a short tour of Germany with the Chantal Orchestra. This was followed in February with a tour of Scandinavia (Denmark, Sweden, Finland and Norway) with The Tremeloes and The Animals. It was a great tour, but we'd essentially spent the entire winter playing in Europe's coldest places.

Spring into the summer was a very busy time for us in the UK. Sadly, though, in the beginning of August, Rob Birrell, our keyboard player, was diagnosed with cancer and had to go undergo chemotherapy. As a temporary replacement we brought in Kevan Lingard, (born October 1958 in Accrington). Kevan started playing piano as a boy and formed his first band, Legend, at fourteen years old. Unfortunately, Robert never made it back into the band, which was upsetting for us, as he was a good friend, not just a great keyboard player and singer.

We didn't have much time to get Kevan rehearsed and up and running before we are on the road again. In August and September, we had plenty of shows in the UK, and then headed off to Denmark with The Searchers and the Bootles, two great bands from Liverpool. We had some good fun joking around with the guys in the other bands. On one occasion, all three groups were patiently sitting on the tour bus waiting for

Frank Allen (of The Searchers) to make an appearance. After five minutes, he made it out through the front door of the hotel, got on to the coach and sat down on the front seat without a hint of apology for keeping us all waiting. Kevan shouted from the back of the coach:

"Frank, have you got your voucher for a free coffee and a croissant at the airport?"

Frank didn't, and asked where he could obtain one. Kevan shouted back that the receptionist at the front desk was handing them out. Frank jumped out of his seat and ran back into the hotel. Of course, everybody else on the coach was in on the joke that there were no free vouchers. After five minutes Frank came out of the hotel after having to queue at the front desk, with an expression of sheer embarrassment on his face. He got back into the coach to a round of loud whistles, shouts and cheers. Frank turned around to face everyone and shouted:

"You're all bastards!"

Most of October and November was taken up with another tour of Australia again, which was followed by a handful of UK dates and a show in Germany. On New Year's Eve we had a disastrous show in Market Deeping, near Peterborough. The gig was held in a gymnasium with chairs and a makeshift dance area. We arrived with no time to sound check, and got changed very quickly, dashing to the stage at the sound of our introduction. We managed to get through one song before the place fell into total darkness, with an interesting accompanying smell of burning electrics. The soundman got out his touch out shone it on the single thirteen-amp plug that was powering absolutely everything…lights, backline and PA. The plug was melted into the mains socket, which in turn had blown the main circuit in the building. End of show, let's go home.

We started 2007 in Germany again…great fun shows but ridiculously cold. Robert Birrell told us that his illness and the chemotherapy he is undergoing would prevent him from making a comeback with the band and suggested that we look for permanent replacement for him. Kevan, who was only a temporary replacement (as we wanted a three-guitar line-up again), is replaced by Graham Pollock. Graham had been in a band called Cavern, not to mention The Eric Haydock Band and Class of 64, to name but a few. But for a variety of reasons things didn't really work out, and after little more than two months, we parted ways with Graham. I phoned Kevan Lingard up and asked him if he'd like his job back permanently, and he was happy to re-join.

In June we did what's called a 'booze cruise' a duty-free cruise that went from Oslo, Norway, to Kiel in Germany. It's two days of fun, and the seafood is superb in the restaurants. We did the same cruise again in September, and similarly, half of the passengers spent most of the trip pissed out of their heads. In between the two cruises though, we managed to squeeze in a month-long tour of Australia.

October was spent in Scandinavian climes on The Golden Sixties Tour with The Tremeloes and The Animals. That show took us to Sweden, Norway and Finland. At the end of October, we went to France to record a TV show about all things 1966. We were there to play No Milk Today, which was a huge hit in France in that year. The show also featured a lot of people and personalities that were famous in France in 1966. The one I remember vividly was the cyclist who won the Tour De France. This guy was probably seventy, so the people in the make-up department stuck Sellotape to both sides of his face, to tidy up some wrinkles, before applying makeup over the Sellotape. As he came out of the makeup room, I told the lads there was no way in Hell they were going to do that to me. When I sat down in front of the mirror and looked at the makeup girl, she must have read my mind and said: "you're okay, next."

In November we were back in Denmark with The Tremeloes and The Bootles for six days. Also, in November an album by Wenche Hartmann, entitled Dance The Night Away, was released. It included a recording of There's A Kind Of Hush, a duet between Wenche Hartmann and Geoff Foot. We'd recorded the song in Australia in August and the file was sent to Denmark where Wenche added her vocal to it. It turned out really good.

In November we did a show in Geneva and Geoff and I went to see the world-famous Jet d'Eau on Lake Geneva. If you're old enough, you might remember it being the huge fountain that was in the opening titles to 60s TV show The Champions. In the afternoon we found a lovely café at the side of the lake so we decided to stop for a coffee. It was a great cup of coffee…and so it should have been at nine pounds a cup! Well at least we can say that we were ripped off in one of the most fabulous places in the world.

The last show of the year was Casino De Paris in Paris, France. Kevan and Geoff went to see the Eiffel Tower and took a photo of it, but I gave it a miss as I had been up the tower in the 60s and swore, I would never do it again. The thing I mostly dislike about the Eiffel Tower is that you can look down through the middle with absolutely nothing underneath you. Even writing about it makes my legs go funny. I remember having the same feeling going up to the top of the World Trade Centre, the Statue of Liberty and the Empire State Building. Especially after my vertigo episode, I think the Blackpool Tower is probably my limit.

In January 2008 we performed on a Danish TV show called Top Charlie where we played There's A Kind of Hush (the duet version recorded by Wenche Hartmann and Geoff Foot). We also did an unplugged version of No Milk Today and then Geoff did a nice interview with the host. In April we had a surprise chart comeback when No Milk Today was used in a TV advertisement for the Norwegian milk company Tine. It had been 42 years since the song was No. 1 in Norway (in 1966), and here we were - based on digital downloads – peaking at No 4, and in the charts for 17 weeks, the song's progress only being beaten by Duffy, Madonna and Maria Haukaas Storeng, which was Norway's Eurovision Song Contest Entry.

On June 9th we played at The Amphitheatre in Afula, Israel, which was very scary indeed as about once an hour you could hear explosions in the distance, and it seemed that absolutely everybody was carrying a gun. We were on with

The Animals and Marmalade and I can tell you I was glad to get home after this show.

Back to the USA, and as per my expensive agreement with Peter, we were billed as 'Herman's Hermits Starring Barry Whitwam'. It was only for one week. We'd lost a lot of American work as Peter's agents, Paradise Artists (who booked most of the 60s groups in the USA) would tell promoters that if they wanted to book popular American 60s groups, they would have to book Peter Noone. For this reason, a lot of the established gigs and tours we had in North America started to dry up… thank goodness for Australian tours.

The next tour in Australian ran from mid-August to mid-September, a gruelling six days a week. We were playing at RSL clubs, which are very large clubs with slot machines, and they all have concert rooms that usually hold over a thousand people, as well as theatres and entertainment centres. They are very similar to American casinos.

There was sadness in October when Robert Birrell died at the age of 59, after a two-year battle with cancer. He was a lovely man and great fun to be with on tour, as well as being a fabulous musician. To this day we reminisce about Rob, and laugh at the stories he would tell.

January to July of 2009 was spent on the usual roundabout of UK and European shows. July 7th saw us head back to the States for another US tour organised by Julie Steddom-Smith. On one of the dates, we were booked for a big show at The National Opera House in Richmond, Virginia. The opera house had been bought and restored by a millionaire benefactor, who turned out to be a really nice guy. He had booked Herman's Hermits Starring Barry Whitwam, Billy J Kramer, Joey Molland & Badfinger, Mike Pender's Searchers, Clem Curtis & the Foundations, and Wayne Fontana and the Mindbenders. In the end, three of the acts had to pull out of the show, starting with Billy J Kramer. Peter Noone had heard that Billy was on the show and told him that if he did the show with me, Billy would never work with Peter Noone again. Billy's wife, Roni, telephoned the promoter and told him to cancel Herman's Hermits. The promoter told her in no uncertain terms that she wouldn't dictate to him who he could and couldn't book for his shows, so he cancelled Billy. Next up, Clem Curtis went to the American embassy in London to get his visa to enter the USA. Clem had filled in his form and, rather foolishly, when asked the question "have you ever been arrested?" ticked the box that said 'Yes'. When interviewed by the visa officer, he was asked what he was arrested for, to which Clem replies:

"Attempted murder of my wife".

"And that's why you won't be going America," replied the officer.

And the only way to complete a story like this is to add some Wayne Fontana. Those that ever knew him will attest to what a unique character he was. Wayne arrived at JFK airport the day before the show, and was waiting in line at immigration. Eventually Wayne stepped up to the counter, explained why he was in the States and satisfied all the other questions from the immigration officer. But when the officer told Wayne to look into the camera, and informs him that he would need to take his fingerprints as well, Wayne recoiled and stated that he wouldn't do either.

"I'm sorry but I won't do that. I'm a member of the universe," said Wayne.

"Beg pardon?" replied the officer, "you're a what now?"

"A member of the universe," Wayne repeated.

"Fine," said the officer, "go and stand over by that wall and wait for another officer to see you."

Two hours later Wayne was on a plane heading back to Manchester.

So now, as there are three fewer artists on the show, the producer (who was also planning to make a DVD of the show) says we will now perform up to one and a half hours, which we obligingly did. To this very day though, I have no idea what happened to the recordings and video.

Our agent in Wisconsin, John Mangold of Talent Associates, sent out all the advertising for the upcoming tour. The billing was to say 'Herman's Hermits starring Barry Whitwam', which was to be all the same size lettering and the same colour. Well probably 75% of the advertising at the shows was wrong in some way or another, and I think it was Waukesha County Fair that had a small billboard, and there was only enough room for 'Herman's Hermits Starring BW'. There was also an advert in the one of the local papers showing Peter Noone's image. I can't remember exactly when Peter Noone filed a lawsuit in the Federal Court of California against myself, John Mangold, Julie Steddom-Smith, and the rest of the band, but he did, and there'll be more about that little nightmare later.

In September we began a five-week tour of Australia, again starting in Twin Towns RSL Club, Coolongatta, (one of the best places to put on a show in the world), before making our way down the coast to Sydney, where we played a show at South Sydney Juniors League Club. It's a great venue but for a drummer it's rather uncomfortable as the air conditioning unit for the whole concert hall is immediately above the drum riser, and is never turned off. At the front of the stage, where the rest of the band is positioned, it's about ninety degrees, but on the drum riser it's a little above freezing. Every time we've played there, I've come away with a severe cold, which one time turned into bronchitis. One time we were there; I asked a stagehand to put two electric fan heaters each side of the drum kit. I would always wear a T-Shirt under my stage clothes and often wore a scarf. During the interludes in the show where I would go to the front of the stage and chat to the audience, the heat from spotlights would soon have steam rising from me…like a race horse after a winter meeting.

While we were in Australia, there was a new DVD release called Listen People 1964-1969 featuring 22 complete songs with stories by myself, Karl Green, Keith Hopwood and Peter Noone. This DVD was one of many released in the British Invasion series, produced by Reelin' In The Years Productions.

The rest of the year was spent around the UK, Denmark, Sweden, Germany and France. Our last show of the year, on 20th December, was in Mansfield at a very big Walker's bingo club. Everything got off to a great start, until our sixth song, when our PA system blew up in a cloud of smoke. We stayed on the stage hoping that our soundman could get it working again, but he couldn't, and after five minutes we had to admit defeat and left the stage. What a way to end the year. Two weeks later though I got a cheque in the post for the full, agreed fee, which I thought was very nice indeed.

January the 15th...what a way to start 2010. We were booked to play a show at the Grand Burstin Hotel in Folkestone for a new agent that we'd never worked for before. I had booked a PA system with a guy who had done sound for us before. He was supposed to arrive at the venue at five o'clock to set up, but by eight o'clock he was still a no-show. The agent is not pleased and I'm not happy with the way it's turning out. On the show with us are two tribute acts using their own small PA systems, so we asked them if they could link up their systems together and make one big one, which would probably be big enough for the job. They very kindly said yes and saved the night, or so I thought. When the last tribute act had finished, we were all on the stage in blackout attempting to set the stage for our performance. While we were making these adjustments, a man came to me and asked if I was in the band. I replied that I was and, handing me a parcel, he said; "this for you".

I thanked him and put it down on the floor until I'd finished what I was doing. It was about the size of a telephone directory, but in the dark, I couldn't see what was written on the front, so I waited until I was in the relative light of the dressing room, which was just to the side of the stage. There in bold letters across the front it said 'The Federal Court of California', and there on the second page was my name and those of everyone else in the band. We had been sued. While we were all in a state of shock, the compere announced us onto the stage. To this day I can't remember what the show was like as we were all gobsmacked. With no sound check, nobody to mix the sound for us, and our newfound consternation, it's probably fair to imagine we weren't at our best, and it was little wonder that the agent never booked the band again.

The next day, after several telephone calls, I finally got through to the soundman I had booked. He told me that he'd had his van and PA stolen a week before. When I asked him why he didn't inform me of this, he made some other excuse about his mobile phone being stolen as well. What I said next can't be printed, but needless to say, I've never used the services of this gentleman since.

The next day on the way to North Wales, I told the other band members that I would take care of all lawyer's fees and I implored them to try not to worry too much as I would get it sorted. It was the same as the last time Noone sued me in the Federal Court…you have 28 days to respond or you lose by default and you have to pay all the other party's costs. This time the case went on for about three years, but I'll tell you later how it went.

As you can imagine, not only did Herman's Hermits not tour the USA in 2010, but we haven't been back since for fear of legal action. Thankfully, thanks to demand and some good agents, Australia had taken the place of the USA in our calendar, and the money for Australian tours has proved to be far better. I think what must have pissed Peter Noone off the most was the fact that I owned the Herman's Hermits Trade Mark in Australia, New Zealand, Europe and the UK. And it probably irked him that he only played 20 shows in 2009, whilst we played 110 all around the world.

We went to Australia again in September and came straight back to the UK to start The Sensational Sixties Experience. This was a 42-date theatre tour organised by Stageright Promotions, which was owned by Billy McGregor and Alan Wearmouth. It was a good show and we went on to do eight more years on this tour, hitting over 600 hundred shows in British theatres.

The Sensational Sixties Experience tour was split into two parts – it would begin in September then run into December, then start again at the end of the next January, running to mid/late April. So after the first part of TSSE, amongst other dates, we went to Norway and Sweden for a week with The Tremeloes, a combination that was always good fun. One particular day we were driving into Sweden from Norway and Rick Westwood (from the Tremeloes) was in the Hermits van as we ran a no smoking vehicle. Ricky always made a sandwich at the breakfast buffet (usually cheese) to eat for lunch. With the Swedish border just a mile ahead, I announced in a voice loud enough for everybody to hear:

"Guys...I don't know if you're aware, but you're not allowed to take food across the border into Sweden. It's against the law and the fines are really heavy if you're caught."

Rick was in the front seat and turned around and asked me if it was true. I said it was, especially for cheese. Rick immediately opened his small travel bag and pulled out his carefully wrapped lunch. He had two large cheese sandwiches, which he devoured in about ten seconds flat, nearly choking in the process. Of course, everybody was in on the joke except for Rick, and when we stopped at a service area thirty minutes later, we all got our own sandwiches that we'd made at breakfast, and started eating them. It took Rick about ten seconds to realise he'd been had, then spent a few minutes telling us what he thought of us, as we all roared with laughter.

A day later and we were traveling back to Norway after a familiar scene at breakfast time, when we all made a sandwich for the road. I watched Rick make a sausage sandwich and, like before it's very carefully wrapped. Then, while he was at the buffet table getting a refill of tea, I exchanged his sandwich for one I'd made earlier, which was just two slices of bread with no filling. An hour later and at the same border crossing into Norway, and Rick turned around from the front seat and announced: "you bastards won't catch me out again". Ten minutes later at a rest area on the Norwegian side, and all of our sandwiches came out. Once again, we were all in on the joke apart from Rick. We all eagerly watched as he opened his sandwich to find no sausage in it. It took him a few seconds to realise he's been had again. I gave him a minute to express himself before I gave him back his own sandwich.

All good things come in threes, and it's the same with pranks. On the last day of the tour, on our way to the airport to fly home, I said to Geoff, who was sat next to Rick, that it was a good job I'd put all the groups cash into a bank in Sweden to be transferred into my account in Manchester, as you're not allowed to take more than £300 in cash out of the country. I knew full well that Rick was carrying well over £10,000 worth of Swedish currency in his little travel bag. He turned round again from the front seat in pure panic.

"I've got loads more than that in my bag," he declared. I told him they'd confiscate the lot and fine him if he was caught. His face went as white as a sheet as the consequences ran through his mind.

"They might even take you away for questioning and then you'll miss the flight home," I added.

On this occasion I couldn't hold it in any longer and, with the rest of the boys, burst out laughing. For the third time in a week, he called us all bastards. Poor Rick.

In March, MGM remastered the film Hold On, which we'd made in 1966. The new DVD starred Herman's Hermits, Shelley Fabares, Sue Anne Langdon and Herbert Anderson, who'd played the father of Dennis the Menace in the TV series. Also, in the same month MGM released the remastered film Mrs Brown, You've Got A lovely Daughter, Starring Herman's Hermits, Sarah Caldwell, Sheila White, Marjorie Rhodes, Stanley Holloway and Lance Percival.

The beginning of April saw us on tour with Gerry & The Pacemakers in New Zealand, a trip organised by Layton Lillas of the Showcase Entertainment Group and John Woolcott of Playtime Promotions. This was a great tour as I had known Gerry for fifty years and always got on royally with him. The tour was to cover the South Island and the North Island. We started on the South Island at the Civic Theatre in Invercargill, which is the most southerly theatre in the world.

The next stop going south is the Antarctic. The second show was in Christchurch, which was just five weeks after a big earthquake, and it was upsetting to see the town centre almost destroyed. The show was moved to a different venue outside of the town centre. The audience really appreciated us going to Christchurch as we were the first international act to appear there since the earthquake. The whole tour was a sell out on both Islands, and I must say that Layton Lillas and John Woolcott did a superb job organising everything. Since that tour we have become very good friends with Layton and John and toured Australia and New Zealand many times.

After returning to the UK, we fell out with Eddy Carter who was replaced by Mike Harling, who had previously played in a band with Kevan Lingard. Mick's first show with us was in Odense, Denmark, but got off to a rocky start as our flight was delayed, and when we finally arrived in Copenhagen, Mick's and Geoff's guitars were missing. By the time we got to the venue the show had already started so there would be no sound check, and Geoff and Mick had to borrow a bass and lead guitar from other bands. Well, as they say, the show must go on and it did, and went down very well.

After Denmark we had several shows in England and Norway, then we were off down under again for a five-week tour of Australia. The tour didn't go so well for Mick as it turned out that as soon as he walked on stage, he was overcome with terrible nerves, and this affected his playing. Also, for some reason Kevan fell out with Mick which didn't help the atmosphere. I had to tell Kevan on several occasions to go easy on Mick as he wasn't helping to put him at ease on stage. Somewhat inevitably, Mick was replaced not long after our return. Into the vacancy stepped Simon Hough – stage name Simon Van Downham – who joined the band in the third week of the Sensational Sixties Experience tour. Simon was a very good all-rounder...an excellent guitarist and singer, who had played with many name bands over the years. That tour, plus a few one-nighters, took us to the end of the year.

2012 was a very busy year for Herman's Hermits. To kick things off was a tour of German theatres. The tour, organised by Rudi Hauptman, had a billing of Herman's Hermits, Middle of the Road, and Dozy, Beaky, Mick and Tich. It was a strong line-up with plenty of hit records between us. Rudi was a likeable rogue who always managed to be short of money at the end of a tour, but we were always grateful to him for filling or January, especially when there was nothing happening in the UK.

In February we jumped back on The Sensational Sixties Experience tour with The Tremeloes, The Dreamers, and Union Gap UK, a show hosted by Alan Mosca from The Dreamers. This tour would keep us busy until the end of March, visiting theatres all around the UK. Before we would start the next Sensational tour in September, we had a lot of shows to play in England, Holland, Norway and Sweden, not to mention a big tour of Australia and New Zealand. The Australian tour was organised by Richard Brown (Ric Tan Associates) and the New Zealand tour by Layton Lillas. This tour was very tiring as we were doing six shows a week and the traveling in between shows, as always in Australia, was quite gruelling. The last show in Australia was once again at the icebox that was South Sydney Junior's Club. I caught a bad cold again and took to New Zealand.

Back in the UK for another Sensational Sixties Experience tour with around 45 shows to keep us busy. In November, in the middle of this stretch of the tour, Simon Van Downham decided he wanted to quit the band as he was not happy with the way the band was run. Essentially, he told me that he wanted better hotels closer to the theatres – and not Travelodge's or Premier Inns. In hindsight though, it may have been the workload, we've always been a busy band. Simon was replaced by Mike Amatt who was a former member of The Rogues and Sunshine in the 60s (and a group that also featured a certain Geoff Foot). Mike had also played with Shane Fenton, later known as Alvin Stardust. Simon went on to tour with Zoot Money and then joined the Scottish band Big Country on vocals, guitar and harmonica.

Peter Noone had been touring the UK on The Solid Silver Sixties show earlier in the year. Our Sensational Sixties Experience promoter, Billy McGregor, was not that bothered as Peter Noone wasn't permitted to use the name 'Hermits' in his advertising, and his presence in the UK certainly didn't affect our ticket sales.

A few more shows and it's the end of a busy year. We did a show on New Year's Eve in a marquee in the gardens of The Ash Pub, Burton End near Stansted. Tommy and Beverly Sowerby, who owned the pub, looked after us after the show well into the wee small hours. Pat and I became good friends with Tommy and Beverly and found out they had an apartment in Pollenca where Pat and I now go on holiday twice a year. Beverly sadly died in 2020.

No rest for the wicked…we begin 2013 with a five-week tour of Germany with The Rubettes (featuring Bill Hurd) and Dozy, Beaky, Mick and Tich. At the end of this tour, Mike Amatt left us after just a few short months. When you spend as long on the road as we do, and in each other's company all day, every day, any personality clashes explode pretty quickly. Paul Cornwell now replaced Mike Amatt, who went back to doing children's theatre shows, with which he'd had a lot of success in the past. Paul Cornwell was poached from the Union Gap UK group where he played bass guitar, but is an excellent lead guitarist and singer as well.

The Sensational Sixties Experience tour started again on February 16th and ran until March 23rd. One realises how much one has toured when you've played nearly all of the theatres before and stayed at all the same hotels before, and you know exactly where the best places to eat are.

However, it's a different matter in Australia. At the beginning of April we head back down under again, but this time we are going to places I've never been to before, mostly in Victoria and South Australia. If you are into star gazing then inland Australia is the place to go, especially if you are staying away from any towns where there is no light pollution. It's wonderful to go back to your motel after a show, and have a few beers, stare at the Milky Way and watch satellites dance across the sky every few minutes (but always keeping an eye out for snakes and spiders in the grass!). At the end of the Australian tour Pat and I went to our favourite holiday destination, Porto Pollenca, Mallorca, for a three-week holiday. After a fabulous break, it's back on the road.

The first show back was in Germany on a sixties show, but in Germany it's called an Oldie Nacht! We were on with Uriah Heep, Karat, Tony Christie, Dozy, Beaky, Mick and Tich, Racey, and The Firebirds. From experience I've learned that the best thing to do at these kind shows, where there are lots of artists on the bill, is to get on stage as early as possible. It's all very well claiming the top of the bill bragging rights, but at these affairs, going on last that can mean getting on stage at two in the morning. These shows always overrun and who wants to be on stage when half of the audience have gone home? I once saw this happen to Shakin' Stevens in Germany; he insisted on going on last, but what began as a two thousand strong crowd, was down to about two hundred by the time he got on stage. And many of them were asleep.

Another high point in the year's busy touring is a gig in June in Leopoldsburg, Belgium. This annual show is organised by Gery Vanrompaey. Gery looks after all the groups superbly, and consequently is very good friends with a lot of British bands. Gery also comes to England to see some of his favourite bands in concert, especially in Folkestone as it's not far from Belgium via the channel tunnel. The 2013 line-up was Herman's Hermits, New Amen Corner, Steve Ellis of The Love Affair, The Swinging Blue Jeans, and The Troggs. The show starts around eight o'clock in the Complex Excelsior Heppen, which is like a big theatre, and usually goes on until about three in the morning. It's a great show and, unlike some similar gigs, nobody in the audience leaves until it's all over.

In August we played our hometown, Manchester, in a suburb called Urmston. The show was to mark the 50th anniversary of The Beatles playing there. The gig was organised by Peter Killick of Something Good Productions Ltd. The line-up was Herman's Hermits, The Tremeloes, The Chancellors, The Bootleg Beatles, The Rainband, and The Vincents. Mike Sweeney, Manchester's very own radio DJ and a good friend, was the compere.

In August we headed back to Australia again – twice in one year! We did actually tour Australia three times in one year when Lek was alive. We started off on the Sunshine Coast at Caloundra Function Centre, then the next day onto the good old Twin Town RSL Resort, Tweed Head, making our way by road to NSW to finish the tour at the club that likes to freeze the drummers, South Sydney Juniors Club. I survived the sub-zero temperatures yet again, but by now I was learning to dress more thoroughly.

Back home to the Sensational Sixties Experience tour and were told by Billy McGregor, the show's producer, to stop joking around with The New Amen Corner. Any touring musician will tell you that playing jokes on other members of the tour is one of the most efficient ways of passing time…and we all have a lot of time. On one occasion at the New Theatre Hull (which funnily enough is a very old building), the stage has gaps between the planks where the now defunct orchestra pit used to be. The gaps are just wide enough to slide a piece of paper through, where they are conveniently visible to whoever should happen to be on stage. We wrote messages on large pieces of paper while New Amen Corner were on stage playing their set. Our selection off messages ranged from 'the drummer's gay' to 'your zips are undone', to 'sing in tune' to 'get off the stage your rubbish', so, sophisticated humour, as you can tell. Our dressing room was next to the orchestra pit where there was an access door to get to under the stage. When the band started to play their first song, we started to push our messages through the gaps in the stage. Naturally, they were laughing their heads off at this, but strangely, the theatre's stage manager was not amused, and came into our dressing room and caught us red handed. He told us to stop doing that as some people in the front row had complained. When we eventually stopped laughing and went back into our dressing room, just in time for Alan Wearmouth to come in and tell us that Billy was on his way down, and was blazing mad. I told everyone to get out of the dressing room announcing that Billy wouldn't fire me so get out and I'll take the blame. Just as everyone had cleared out Billy comes rushing in and shouted:

"This is not a fucking comedy show, and if any of the audience wants their money back it's coming out of your money!".

He asked me where the rest of the Hermits were. I told him they were in the pub next door.

"So, you did all these signs by yourself did you?" he asked, as I brought out my Tupperware box with his favourite snack – pork pie with English mustard. That did the trick.

"Here Billy," I said, "have some humble pie." He smiled, took a big mouthful and said: "no more jokes". I assured him that I'd stop joking around from now on. Four days later we were playing Fairfield Hall, Croydon, which was the penultimate night of the tour, and it was time for another prank. A few days before Croydon I had gone into a joke shop and bought a blow-up ballerina outfit, and it didn't take long for me to find a use for it. While The New Amen Corner were playing their set, Geoff Foot, (hidden inside the costume) pirouetted onto the stage and started messing about next to Glen Leon, the lead singer with the NAC. The audience, who had been a bit quiet until now, suddenly came to life, and many of them took out their cameras to snap this funny episode. Chris Farlowe, who was due on shortly, said to the stage manager that he'd prefer if they got that woman off the stage before he started his set. Billy McGregor went ballistic, and wanted to know who the fat mystery ballerina was, but not many of the cast knew it was Geoff. I think Billy suspected the Hermits were behind it, but couldn't prove it.

The last night of the tour was at The Marina Theatre in Lowestoft, and the last chance for a joke. Glen Leon decided to put one of those whistling gadgets down my exhaust pipe, but Kevan Lingard saw him do it and took it out. An hour later Glen came into our dressing and asked if we were staying in Lowestoft for the night. I said we were supposed to but I'd had to cancel it because my van was making strange noises, and I would have to order a low-loader to take it back to Manchester. Glen looked a little worried and left the dressing room. He came back ten minutes later and confessed to putting a whistling devise down the van's exhaust pipe and said he was sorry about us traveling back to Manchester and cancelling our hotel. We all started laughing as the joke was on him, and he started laughing as well as he realised, he'd been had big style. The whistling gadget ended up down Billy McGregor's exhaust pipe, to accompany him and Alan on their journey home to Northumberland after the show. I didn't think any more about it until I got a phone call the next day from Billy who told me he'd had to take his car into a BMW garage as there was a whistling sound coming out of his engine, and after two hours of inspection, the mechanic had found that a toy up his exhaust pipe was the culprit. Billy asked me who had done it so that he could deduct three hundred pounds from their money, as that's what the garage had charged him in labour and time spent looking for the problem. He was not pleased. He never found out who actually did it, and my lips are still sealed. Three days later and we were in Germany on a three-week tour, then we finished the year with friends back at The Ash Pub, Stansted for the New Year's Eve bash.

Sometime when I look back on the tours we have done in the past, I'm amazed how I got through some of them. For example, when I consider that the Monkees' 20th Anniversary tour in 1986 was nine months long, I also have to consider that I was only 40 years old. Now here I was on January 2nd 2014, about to start a two-month tour with Dozy, Beaky, Mike and Tich, and The Rubettes (featuring Bill Hurd), at the ripe old age of 68…

But as they say, if you are enjoying your job, you'll never do a day's work in your life. A maxim that even holds up in the chilly depths of a German winter. For some years now, Herman's Hermits have a rule that everybody has their own hotel room. When you spend hours, days, weeks and months in each other's close company (not just on stage but traveling, dining and endless hours of waiting), to have your own space at the end of each day is a godsend, and fairly vital for one's continued mental wellbeing. Well, we made it through the German tour unscathed, and returned to the UK just in time for the spring, and to reconvene the Sensational Sixties Experience Tour, which would keep us busy until mid-April when we headed off to Norway for a tour organised by our old friend Bjorn Terje Brathen, of Artistguiden. For this tour we were playing two different one-hour shows per night, with a twenty-minute interval to sell a few CD's. I must say, I never tire of travelling around Norway; it's such a beautiful country to visit, and there are so many islands and fjords that you need to cross by ferries, that you get to see a lot of stunning scenery when moving from one venue to the next.

Back in the UK in June, and we started to adopt our Norwegian model for our own shows. As we'd stopped going to America in the summer, our diary was filled with UK dates until we headed off for a five-week tour of Australia in August. We kicked off at Twin Town Services Club, Gold Coast, then worked our way down to the drummer fridge at South Sydney Juniors, where I caught my best cold yet, a cold so bad that I ended up paying to see a doctor who prescribed some antibiotics for me, and advised me to take a week off work. Fat chance. The next night we played at Menai, which is a suburb of Sydney. Thankfully, we then had two days off in Sydney, and where possible spent as much time as possible at Manly Beach. The Observer Hotel (the Rocks Bar) was conveniently placed for those waiting for a ferry to Manly. Once on the causeway at Manly, we all went our different ways for shopping and souvenir purchasing, and agreed to meet up again in The New Brighton Pub on the ocean side of Manly Beach for a few more pints, before going for an Indian curry.

There's a great Indian restaurant called the Ashiana, just across the road from the Brighton Pub. The first time I visited the Ashiana, I happened to have some of my homemade onion, paprika, tomato and mango sauce in a Tupperware container (you could smell me coming!). That night, we'd had a superb meal, and the owner became intrigued by the container of sauce that we were dipping our poppadom's into. On our way out I told him that we would be back in exactly one year, to which he promised he would make my onion and mango starter for us. Here we were a year later tucking into said sauce, and other wonders. I suppose that makes me a regular customer. By the time we got back on the ferry, we were very full, half pissed (as usual) and grinning like a Cheshire cat.

At the end of the Australian tour, Pat and I went to Pollenca, Mallorca, for a break before starting another Sensational Sixties Experience Tour, with over 50 theatres to visit. With a handful of shows in December, that took us to a relatively relaxing Christmas. I did hear that earlier in the year Karl Green had played a few shows in America, but no doubt Peter had his legal team primed to make sure it wouldn't go any further.

A tour of Germany in January was becoming as certain as Christmas in December, and this time (2015) we were joined by The Equals, Barry Ryan, and Racey. This German tour lasted six weeks and covers a lot of miles by road. We had a lot fun with Racey and have become firm friends since that tour. At the end of February, we reconvened the Sensational Sixties Experience, visiting every corner of the UK with The Swinging Blue Jeans, The Union Gap UK, The Ivy League, Chris Farlowe, Dave Berry and The New Amen Corner, along with The Dreamers' Alan Mosca hosting the show. Thank goodness for Wetherspoons pubs; even in the sparsest of towns, there is nearly always one, and it's usually very close to the theatre. The food is good, they're open all day, and the beer is cheap! The chain has become something of a sanctuary for touring musicians.

The joking and pranking with The New Amen Corner is relentless, and continues for the whole tour. On one occasion we finished our set and went back to our dressing room to find it completely empty. I checked the number on the door...it was the correct room but there was nothing in it. In an identical dressing room one floor above, we found all our clothes had been laid out exactly as they were in the original dressing room. When confronted, Amen Corner said they hadn't a clue what we were talking about, as usual. Another time, while we were stage, they went into our dressing room and placed 380 paper cups full of water between the door and the main part of the room, making it impossible to get into the room without kicking water everywhere, and of course they denied all knowledge of it. At the New Theatre in Hull, they were all stood outside the stage door waiting to see us off. We knew they had done something but couldn't see anything out of place. We drove off in our Volkswagen people carrier and they followed us into the town centre. We stopped at some traffic lights with The New Amen Corner van next to us, and a police car on the other side. Glen Leon was sat on the passenger side of their van and opened his window to tell us there was a lot of noise coming from underneath our van. As we drove off with my window still down, I could hear this terrible clagging sound coming from underneath our van. I slowed down and as they passed us we could see them laughing their heads off. We pulled over to see what was making the noise, and there behind our van was a six-foot long rope with about twelve beer cans and various other metal items attached to it. As we were untying the rope the police car came alongside us…the officers just smiled and shook their heads as they drove off. Another time they got one over on us was at The Embassy Theatre in Skegness. We came out of the stage door after the show to find our van completely covered in toilet paper. A couple of days later we pulled into the Doncaster services on the M18 for a coffee and we saw their van…this was our chance for revenge. So we quickly pulled in next to their van and put empty water bottles on their windscreen wipers and taped them on with duct tape. As we entered the main door of the services, The Corners were coming out. We smiled and watched as they walked to the car park. Much to our horror they got into an identical van to the one we had just trashed…we'd got the wrong van. As they drove off, they saw the van that we'd done the business on, laughed and gave us the finger through the open windows.

There would be plenty of time to get them back on the next tour, which would start in October.

Midway through April and we were back in Denmark and Norway. The Danish part of the tour was organised by Stig Ulrichsen, who we had worked with ever since he took over CB & Ole B. Booking in Randers. The Norwegian stretch was booked and promoted by Bjorn Terje Brathen, and as usually it was fabulously organised. We did six shows in Denmark and four in Norway and although the weather was cold, it was still enjoyable. At the end of May we did a big show in Germany with a lot of acts that had become good mates – Slade, T-Rex, Sailor, Marmalade, The Equals, The Troggs, The Firebirds and Frank Schobel and Band. We had a great laugh with everybody back stage, partly due to the concert catering on the continent being so much better than the UK. A few more shows in England then it was back to Leopoldsburg in Belgium for an outdoor show, booked and organised, again, by Gery Vanrompaey. The show is near the centre of town, and just one hundred yards away from our hotel…it doesn't get any better than that.

From August 5th to September 7[th,] we were in Australia for a busy tour that started in Perth, Western Australia. We did a few scheduled shows, then played at Friends Restaurant in Cloisters, Perth. The restaurant is run and owned by Clyde & Lesley Bevan, and I have to say it's the best restaurant in Australia in my experience. The stage is very small but that doesn't matter, as the atmosphere in the room is out of this world. The next night we played the Joondalup Resort in Perth and – small world that it is – my old neighbours who lived across the road from me, Dace & Cath France (who had emigrated to Perth) came to see the show. We had a great time reminiscing. After Western Australia we had one show in Adelaide and then, we were supposed to drive to Southport, Queensland, which is over two thousand kilometres by road. But I put my foot down and said we weren't going to travel in Warren Trout's (our tour manager) old van, which was very uncomfortable, all the way to Southport QLD. Instead, we had three days in Adelaide then flew to Brisbane, where Warren Trout met us at the airport in said old van. In hindsight, we should have flown to Brisbane and had three days in Southport.

I fondly remember when we first started touring with Richard Brown Associates many years before. Richard was a hands-on kind of promoter and would do all the driving, help set the stage, make sure the catering was set up in the dressing room, and a hundred other things. He even sold our merchandise before, during and after shows. Unfortunately, Richard got cancer and couldn't be on the road anymore, so he delegated the touring part to Warren Trout, and that's when things started to go downhill. Richard Brown used to hire a twelve-seat bus with plenty of room for everybody, and with air conditioning that always worked. Warren Trout used his own Toyota people carrier (which had seen better days) and, it was at this point in time that I started to contemplate going with another promoter.

So, in Warren Trout's old knacker, we made our way down to Sydney via the South-Sydney-freeze-a-drummer-to-death-centre, and then spent our day off at Manly Beach, following exactly the same routine as we had the year before. Actually, there was one addition to that routine; we'd got hold of some fake twenty-dollar bills, and spent a wonderful hour or so dropping them from the balcony of the Brighton Pub onto the pavement below. It was enormous fun to see people's different methods of picking up a note, and thinking they were twenty dollars richer. Some would look around to see if they were being observed, some would simply stoop and gather inn their stride. But the funniest part was always a few yards down the road when they would take the note out of their pockets to scrutinise their findings, only to discover they'd been had. After that we went for a well-earned curry before heading back to our hotel via the ferry and a train from Circular Quay. It had been another great day off in Manly. Like anybody else, after a month in Australia I like to take a two-week holiday in Majorca.

Straight after the holiday it was back on the road with The Sensational Sixties Experience for another 49 shows with our mates Chris Farlowe, Steve Ellis, Union Gap UK, The New Amen Corner, and The Swinging Blue Jeans. The Corners were at it from night one. While we were on stage, they went into our dressing room and took my car keys, then moved my VW people carrier two hundred yards down the road, before putting my keys back into my pocket. I was just about phone the police to report it stolen when one of the other groups on the show said they had seen my van at the bottom of the road. Very funny…this was war. The next day I had an hour off in the next town we were playing, so I went into town and found a sex shop. After a few awkward moments with the young lady that worked there, and my protestations that 'it wasn't for me', I asked for a blow-up doll.

"Black or white?" she asked.

"It's not for me. Which one is the cheapest?" I replied.

Apparently, it was the black one, and at just twenty-five pounds, she had a sale. On the way out she said: "have fun", and again I said: "it's not for me!" She merely smiled as I walked out, red-faced. That night while Amen Corner were on stage, I took their van keys and the blow-up doll out to their van, opened the driver's door, blew the doll up, put some underpants on her, then placed her in the driving seat with the hands on the steering wheel. Naturally, I took a photo with my phone. The next thing was to let the air out of the doll, put the keys back in Amen Corner's dressing room, and put the photo on Facebook with the caption, 'Amen Corner's new roadie'. They have never said a word about it to this day. We finished the tour and did several shows on our own and that concluded 2015.

January 2016 saw us on the road with what was becoming a customary tour of Germany, this time travelling with The Tremeloes, Vanity Fair, Ohio Express and Tony Christie. The Tremeloes played a good joke on me one night at the end of our song Something Is Happening. What normally happens at the end of the song is that I throw a drumstick high into the air and miss-catch it on purpose. Geoff Foot then says to the audience: "Did he catch it?", and they all shout say "no!". So on this occasion I threw my stick high, and to my surprise I look up to see dozens and dozens of sticks descending on me. It turns out that everybody backstage had simultaneously thrown several hundred pretzel sticks in the air, which all landed on my drums. It was a showstopper and the audience loved it. I don't think there were any pretzels left in town to buy that night.

We got Vanity Fair one-night, big style. In the intermission, we put a pipe cleaner down Bernie Hagley's penny whistle. Halfway through their set, Bernie set off into a long monologue about how he played the penny whistle on the intro to the hit record Hitchin' a Ride. When he finished talking, he put the penny whistle in his mouth and started playing the intro, which of course, was nothing like the record. He stops playing and apologised to the audience before trying again. Sounding just as bad, he again stopped and began examining the inside of the penny whistle. Seeing something was stuck inside it he picked up his spare one, which we had given the same treatment. We were at the side of the stage watching as he tried again with the same result...a truly horrendous sound. He stopped and looked down the whistle to see something stuck in it and, giving it a good shake, the pipe cleaner came flying out. Off microphone he said: "bloody Hermits", or words to that effect. Thankfully, the whole thing was videoed, and I still laugh when I watch it.

At the end of the German tour, I was told the very sad news that Chris Finley had died of a heart attack. Chris, an ex-Hermit who played in the band for a couple of years between 1973 -1974, was a great bass guitarist and keyboard player. After leaving the band he was involved with many bands and artists on the Liverpool music scene including Liverpool

Express, Supercharge, Mike McCartney, Beryl Marsden and The Merseybeats.

After Germany we hooked up with the Sensational Sixties Tour for two months before a short tour of Norway and Denmark, after which we headed out to Leopoldsburg, Belgium, for an open-air concert organized by our old friend Gery Vanrompaey. The show is a great success as always.

On July 23rd I held my 70th birthday bash at the Marriott Manchester Airport Hotel. The Ivy League put on a fabulous show for me, my guests talked about them for weeks. On July 28th we were on our way to Australia again for what turned out to be the worst tour of my life. Warren Trout was on form booking some the worst motels I have stayed in in over 50 years, but he blamed Richard Brown for booking the motels. The places we stayed seemed to be competing with each other in the filth and squalor stakes. Geoff and Sharon (Geoff's fiancé) always have a double room, but on one occasion they were given a key to a room so small that you couldn't get the door open enough to get the luggage in, as the door hit the bed. To use a group term…they were shit holes.

One night at the venue, Warren Trout exceled himself when he set up the drums on a riser, using a 6'x6' piece of linen instead of carpet. After the first ten seconds of the first song, the bass drum started to slide towards the edge of the rostrum, so I constantly had to pull back the bass drum to stop it falling off the riser. Warren Trout was nowhere to be seen while this was going on, and I was beginning to lose my patience. I looked down at my set list and noticed the medley was next, which was six consecutive songs with no breaks. I felt like doing a Keith Moon and kicking the drum off the riser. I shouted to Geoff that we would have to finish the first set as the drums were no longer playable, so Geoff made an announcement that we would take a short break for technical reasons, and would be right back. I went off stage into the dressing room, which was on the side of the stage, to find Warren Trout fast asleep on a settee. What I said to him is unprintable, but the result was that he went off to find a piece of carpet. He came back with three different sized pieces of carpet, which had to be taped together. That same night after the show we were signing autographs and selling CDs in the foyer...the merchandise sales were organized by Warren and Sharon. Kevan chose this moment to utter his unacceptable opinions of Sharon to Geoff, which, needless to say, nearly ended in blows, although foreheads did touch the way footballers sometimes do when they're a little cross. Sharon does a fine job selling CDs, and Kevan had no problem taking his share of the CD money every day, but his attitude towards Sharon was out of order. The whole episode was unacceptable in my book. The next morning before we got into Warren's van for the next uncomfortable trip to the next town, I got everybody into my room and read the riot act out. I said anybody fighting on this tour or any other will be on the next flight home, and I told Kevan to take off his agent's hat and be a part of the band, as he'd been trying to sell Warren Trout UK bands to tour Australia. For some reason, Keven had told Paul Cornwell that they were going to be replaced after this tour by

Glen Leon and Jules Benjamin from The New Amen Corner…God only knows where that idea came from.

    The PA engineer wasn't making matters better, as he was smoking joints and drinking heavily until all hours of the night. When we checked into motels, Geoff and I always got rooms on the other side of the motel away from Kevan and Paul. Things had to change so I phoned Richard Brown our agent and told him that if the transport situation didn't change then I was going to look for a new agent. He told me that Warren was charging him the same as hiring a new twelve-seater air-conditioned bus, yet there we were in Warren's clapped-out Toyota people carrier. Richard said things would improve for the next tour. A few days later I phoned Tony Brady (The Searchers' Australian promoter) and he said he would love to tour Herman's Hermits in Australia. I told Geoff the next day, and we both agreed it was a good backup, just in case. The last show on the tour was at Friends Restaurant in Perth, where we were booked for two days, and they were both sold out, which was a lovely way to end the worst tour I have ever been on.

    We caught the red eye out of Perth which meant I'd had no sleep, but I was very much looking forward to seeing a few of the latest films, then having a good sleep at some point within the following twenty-eight hours of flying. After picking up my luggage at Manchester airport, I went over to Kevan and Paul to say goodbye, and to inform them that it had been the worst tour I'd ever been on in fifty-two years, and that they had better get used to Sharon as she was going to be on all the tours selling merchandise.

"All tours? Then I resign," shouted Kevan. "Do you want that in writing?"

"Yes please," I replied. I then turned to Paul.

"And what do you want to do?" I asked. He said he would still like to be in the band, if it was all right with me. I said yes and told him to have a good holiday.

Kevan Lingard was replaced by Paul Robinson (nicknamed Robbo), who had worked with a variety of acts including Paper Lace and The Meatloaf Story. Robbo's first gig was at Lakeside Coastal Village, Hayling Island and then got his first taste of The Sensational Sixties Experience tour from early October until mid-December. Robbo was a lovely guy, but just didn't fit in with rest of the band, and left on December 16th after a show at The Platform, Morecambe.

In January 2017, Paul was replayed by Tony Hancox who had played keyboards since seven years old, and studied at the London College of music, whilst doing session work for bands, radio and television.

We had a few shows on our own before joining up with another Sensational Sixties Experience tour, this time with The Swinging Blues, The Ivy League, The Merseybeats, The Fortunes, The New Amen Corner and Chris Farlowe, and as ever, the show was hosted by Alan Mosca. On this tour I had mastered the art of flying a drone and planned to fly it over The New Amen Corner as they played. I stood waiting in the wings of the Alexander Theatre in Birmingham ready to buzz Jacko Howson, their drummer. I had the drone about twelve feet in the air ready to make my attack on him when Alan Wearmouth came up behind me and asked what I was playing at. I said "nothing" as the drone crashed to the floor behind me. "Maybe next time," I muttered as I walked away.

As usual there were plenty of jokes played on The New Amen Corner, and vice versa. At one time on the tour they bought a new, large red van, so we took a photo of it with an iPhone and went to work on it in a paint shop app. By the time we'd finished it had a lovely Royal Mail logo on it. It was posted on Facebook immediately. As usual, we didn't get any response from them. We finished the tour in April and had five days off before going to Denmark and Norway for twelve days, finishing off on a Stena Saga cruise from Oslo to Copenhagen. As I've said before, the Norwegians really know how to cook seafood, so I was in my element.

From May to July, we had plenty of shows around the UK as well as another visit to Leopoldsburg, Belgium, to play another open-air show for Gery Vanrompaey. From July 17th to August 1[st,] we toured New Zealand for Layton Lillas of Showcase Group. Layton is a kiwi and certainly knows how to run a tour, and we ended being solid friends by the time we'd finished touring the North and South Islands.

A funny thing happened at the beginning of the tour… when the PA company (owned by Scott Williams) arrived from Hamilton on the North Island, they opened the back doors of their large van and out jumped a black cat. Scott recognized it as his next-door neighbour's cat, which must have jumped in the back when they were loading their system up. It was a lovely cat and was on tour with us for about a week before Layton had it driven back to its owners in

Hamilton. The cat made the front page of the newspapers in Hamilton and went worldwide on the internet.

In the Wellington airport car park two hours before we left the country to fly to Australia for our last tour with Warren Trout and Richard Brown, I made a deal with Layton to organise our tours of Australia and New Zealand the following year.

We landed in Brisbane and were met by Warren who, to our surprise, had a new(ish) people carrier. It was the same make and colour, but nowhere near as old. However, this van eventually broke down too in Melbourne, and he had to have it shipped back to Warwick, Queensland, and hire a twelve-seater van. Once again, we played our favourite venue, the Twin Town Services Club, which has a twelve hundred capacity concert room, which we fill year on year. The usual visit to South Sydney drummer freezing club was followed, as usual, with a trip to Manly Beach for a few pints and a curry at the usual restaurant. Once again, the tour finished at Friends Restaurant in Perth, before the long flight home. After such hardship, the only medicine was to take a three-week holiday with Pat in Mallorca.

Before we could start another Sensational Sixties Experience tour we had three shows in Bonn, Germany, one of which was recorded for a TV show. The opening stretch of the SSE tour ran from October 6th to December 9th and, along with Herman's Hermits, featured Mike Pender, Chris Farlowe, The Fortunes, Mike d'Abo and The New Amen Corner. It was a very busy tour, but enormous fun.

As the beginning of 2018 showed, we were getting into a bit of a routine along the lines of…January to April the Sensational Sixties Experience, then Norway and Denmark until mid-May, a three-week holiday in Mallorca, then off to Leopoldsburg in Belgium. The first half of the summer was spent playing one-nighters around the UK, with a few shows in Germany. But this year on the 1st of August we flew to Australia to start a tour of Australia and New Zealand that had been organised by Layton Lillas. The whole tour was in theatres and arts centres, and, as he had done the year before in New Zealand, Layton did a superb job and laid on a memorable and enjoyable tour. For transportation we had two Kia Caravelles (which were incredibly comfortable to travel in), the equipment was of a high quality, and the hotels were first rate. As I've always said…give us the tools and we'll finish the job. We had a full tour booked, and it ran beautifully. We also got to do three shows in Tasmania before we flew back to The Palms at Crown in Melbourne, which is a superb venue to play. In the second half of the show we were playing a tune called Let There Be Drums originally by Sandy Nelson. Halfway through the tune is the cue for the boys to leave the stage, then I take a drum solo for about four minutes. The lighting man went to town lighting up me and my kit; it looked like a flying saucer landing on the stage. I spoke to him after the show and he said how much he'd enjoyed lighting it up. A few weeks later somebody uploaded it to YouTube and it looked fantastic. After Australia we travelled down to The South Island of New Zealand, which is a lovely place to visit and play. We played eight theatre shows which all went down very well indeed.

Straight after New Zealand it was back home, and the next day Pat and I take a two-week holiday to…you guessed it… Mallorca! It was the same hotel, the same room and the same restaurants as ever, but we love it. Come October and we were back onto the next Sensation Sixties Experience tour, joining The Dakotas, The Fourmost, Mike d'Abo, Mike Pender, Chris Farlowe, The Swinging Blue Jeans and The New Amen Corner. That took us to the beginning of December, and with a handful of shows in the UK and one in Essen, Germany, it was another year gone.

2019 was looking like a great year. In the diary was the second phase of the Sensational Sixties Experience tour (which would be our last of a long run with Stageright Promotions), a tour of Norway and Denmark, another Australian tour organised by Layton Lillas and then the Sixties Gold tour promoted by Robert Pratt and Alan Field. Plus we had three big shows booked in Germany and a variety of other shows in the UK. However, in May, the week between the end of the Danish tour and our first show at the Whitby Sixties weekend, it all kicked off with a massive argument between Geoff and Paul over the transport for the next Australian tour. The transport arrangements were all in place but Paul didn't like them, and Paul and his partner, Cindy, didn't like the fact that Geoff's partner Sharon was on tour with us more than she was. Paul and Cindy made phone calls and sent texts that were totally out of order, and I decided I wasn't going to put up with such bad feeling in my band. I know some of the phone calls were alcohol induced, but that's all I'm going to say on the matter. I made the decision not to take Paul and Cindy to Australia at all; I wasn't prepared to allow the situation to erupt on the road like it had before. So after the show at Whitby, I informed Paul that that was his last show with Herman's Hermits. I don't think he'd realised that what he had said and done would get him the sack, but it did.

The next day we had our last show on the Sensational Sixties tour, which was in Chatham. We had to go via Manchester to pick up Graham Lee who said he would stand in on lead guitar for that show. We had three shows booked in Germany ten days later but Graham said he couldn't do them as he was scheduled to have an operation on one of his eyes in that period. After a great deal of thought and a few phone calls, Beaky, from Dozy, Beaky Mick and Tich suggested I call Ray Frost, who had been playing with The Rubettes. We had toured with The Rubettes a couple of years before, so we knew each other well. I phoned him immediately. Ray lives in Spain, but that wouldn't be a problem as the shows were in Germany, and he could travel to Germany from Spain just as easily as we could travel to Germany from the UK. He said he would love to give it a try so I sent him the list of songs, keys, and some live recordings of our set. Ten days later Ray, Tony, Geoff and I met up at the hotel we were staying at near the first venue in Thale, Germany, where we had about an hour rehearsing the show in my hotel room before setting off for the show.

Ray did a fantastic job learning the songs and the first show went down a storm, as did the other two. We still had the problem of finding a permanent lead guitarist/vocalist to replace Paul Cornwell. Tony said he knew a guitarist who he used to play in a band with a good few years ago – Duncan Keith – so in for a penny in for a pound. I organised a rehearsal/audition in a studio in Stoke on Trent. He wasn't bad but he was very keen…he wrote everything down in a book as we went along. We did over thirty-two hours of rehearsal but he was still making lots of mistakes, it just wasn't getting any better, but we were committed now and we had to get through Australia somehow.

When we finally got to Australia, our promoter Layton Lillas said that Duncan was making too many mistakes. I said it would get better, but it didn't. It was difficult but we managed to get through the tour, although Layton was not very happy to say the least. At Manchester Airport I had to tell Duncan that his days with Herman's Hermits were over, and in fairness, he said he was expecting something like that. Looking back now I think Duncan did a fine job under the pressure he was under. As soon as I got home I telephoned Ray Frost in Spain to see if he was available to do The Sixties Gold tour, which was starting on 27th September, as he had done such a good job for us in Germany in July. In hindsight, I have no idea why I didn't ask Ray to do the Australian tour instead of Duncan. Anyway, Ray was now a full time Hermit and when possible, got back to Spain, sometimes just for a couple of days when there was a break in the tour. The tour was a great success and was rebooked for 2020.

Like 2019, 2020 was going to be a great year for the band as we had a nice variety of exiting things filling the diary; these included a tour of Norway, An Evening With Herman's Hermits tour booked in 59 theatres, a tour of Australia booked, and a repeat slot booked on the Sixties Gold tour. But 2020 went wrong for very different reasons. On 17th March, the whole country went into lockdown, and like every single one of our musician friends, the rest of the year's diary evaporated into thin air. A few days later, Layton Lillas, our Australian promoter, phoned to say that the Australian tour was postponed. It was rearranged for 2021, before being moved again to 2022, and then that tour was cancelled. In 2020 we played a total of 21 shows in the UK and 5 in Norway. 26 gigs. It was the fewest number of shows I'd played in a calendar year for 60 years.

In 2021 Geoff said that he wanted to leave the band at the end of the year as he was going to immigrate to Australia with his wife Sharon, who is Australian. So I phoned Jules Benjamin, a multi-talented musician who I have known for a long time, and he said he would be delighted to join. I sent him all the songs we did in our show, which was more than thirty songs. Two months later Geoff changed his mind and said he didn't want to leave the band now. I had the unpleasant job of phoning Jules to tell him that Geoff wasn't leaving now and he was no longer needed. Jules was gutted.

A few months later Geoff decided he was going to leave for good this time so I made some enquiries for a lead singer that could bass guitar. Within a few days I'd spoken to Lee Clarkson from the Fourmost, and he gave me the number of

Jamie Thurston, who, at the time was playing with the Tornados. I phoned Jamie up and he said he would love to audition for the job. I sent him five songs to learn and I arranged an audition in a studio in Stoke-on-Trent. A week later Tony Hancox (keyboard player) got together with Jamie, who passed the audition with flying colours

As of May 2023, the band has made some changes in personnel. Geoff Foot is no longer in the band. In 2022 he had an injury to his leg and got deep vein thrombosis and had to miss a few shows. He still suffers with it today. John Summerton, who was playing with Gerry's Pacemakers had seen us so many times that it was straightforward for him to stay in for Geoff. The logistics of touring were getting complicated, what with Geoff not knowing whether or not he'd be fit enough for various long journeys, and travels abroad; promoters usually book tickets for flights and make other arrangements well before they happen. It got to the stage where Geoff conceded that the situation was far from ideal, what with so many travel arrangements being subject to last minute changes, so we agreed on his last date with the band. Saturday 14th of January 2023, in sunny Minehead, was Geoff's last gig as a Hermit, after 34 years of distinguished service. With that settled, I invited John Summerton to join Herman's Hermits as a full-time member, to which he enthusiastically agreed. At that time, the lineup consisted of me on drums, Jamie on bass guitar and lead vocals, Tony Hancox on keyboards and vocals, and John Summerton on lead guitar and lead vocals.

I had already begun booking shows for the 60th Anniversary Tour in 2024. However, as the year drew to a close, the band underwent yet another change in personnel, with Tony Young replacing Tony Hancox on keyboards and vocals. I must say, with this new lineup, the band has never sounded better.

12

Heartbeat for the family

Being married to a full-time musician who travels the world is not for every girl, and perhaps because of that, my first marriage lasted seventeen years. Her name was Dale and we had two lovely children, Emma and Richard, who are both married with families of their own, as well as having very successful careers and businesses.

Dale was a nurse when we first meet at the Beachcomber Club in Bolton, before our world-domination began! She was working three weeks on night shifts, then three weeks on day shifts, and like a lot of nurses would take tablets to keep awake while on the night shifts, and different tablets to help sleep during the days off. Unfortunately, she got addicted to prescription drugs. The second time I met her was after the release of our first record, I'm Into Something Good. I told her that I remembered seeing her six months earlier at the Beachcomber. We got chatting and started seeing each other on and off when I had a day off, which was not often. My Dad confided in me that he thought there was something wrong with her. She would come round to stay at our house on weekends when I was away with the band, and Dad noticed that Dale would go to bed on a Friday night and not come downstairs until Sunday morning. After a while I decided that having a girlfriend was not for me, as I was having a great time with the band and going out with lads for drinks on my days off. So, one night I went round to her house and said I didn't won't to go out with her any more, and that it was over. The next day my Mum asked me what had happened because Dale's mother had been on the phone saying she was suicidal. My mother instructed me to get round there and immediately make up with her, which I did.

A year later we were engaged. I had a Saturday off and I was going to tell my dad of my plans. He used to lie in late on a Saturday morning, so I thought this was a good time to tell him. I went into his bedroom, and he was sleeping on his side facing me. I said "Dad I've got some great news". He opened his eyes and I told him I was getting engaged to Dale, to which he just turned over and went back to sleep. I could write another book about my time with Dale, and her problems. She passed away at the age of fifty-two with cancer. The chemotherapy didn't work well as her immune system was basically shot from taking drugs over the previous twenty-five years.

A year before we got divorced, I met Pat, my wife now, and for the last thirty-three years. Pat had a German Shepard she used to walk home after dropping her son (Jono) off at the same school that my son, Richard, went to, and we would walk together talking and I would tell her daft jokes. We would pass my house to get to where Pat lived, and I knew Dale wouldn't be up as she usually slept in until ten thirty, and would not be looking out of the bedroom window. The third time we were walking across the playing fields, Pat's Germany Shepard attacked my golden retriever, Mr Chips, who ran off and went home on his own. When I got to my house Mr Chips was sitting by the front door, which I was thankful for. The next morning when it was time to take Richard to school I called Mr Chips, like I always did, but he wouldn't come up to me to have his lead put on. He would not go outside for the walk to school, so I had to carry him about one hundred yards down the street then put him down and put the lead round his neck. Mr Chips was my excuse for coming home from school late so I had to carry him down the street every day so he would walk to school with Richard and I. After a few weeks I was getting some strange looks from other parents. I think they thought - there's that nutty drummer carrying his golden retriever to school.

A year after I started seeing Pat, I decided to get a divorce from Dale. A long story short, I got custody of Emma and Richard and sold the family home, and after paying off the mortgage I split the proceeds fifty-fifty with Dale. With my share of the money, I bought Pat's husband's share of their house and moved in. Emma went to live with Dale but after a few months came to live with Pat and I. Four months later Emma went to college in Bedford to become a teacher. Pat had her own business shipping animals and pets around the world from the Manchester cargo centre which kept her busy while I was away on tour. Whenever possible Pat would join me on tour, especially when we did cruises on the Cunard Line. Once we went all the way to Istanbul, which took in a lot of stops along the way. It was the first time the QE2 had gone to Istanbul. I went into a leather shop in the bazaar and bought a lovely leather peak cap like Rudolf Nureyev, the famous male ballerina. The first time I put it on Pat said, "and where do you think you're going to wear that?"

Pat and I have had some wonderful times cruising the world, as well as on tours in the USA and Europe.

While I was at home between tours, I would help Pat out with collections of various animals. On one occasion I had to pick up two sheep from a farm. They were being exported to Canada, along with other pets belonging to a family who had emigrated there. It seemed like a straightforward job. Pat had been sent the measurements of the sheep and had boxes made for them. One of the sheep was very large and the other was much smaller. I had lined up the boxes outside of the barn where the sheep had been kept over-night waiting for transportation to the airport. It was time to get the sheep into the boxes, so I opened the barn door, and the small sheep made a run for the big box, closely followed by the big sheep. I now have two sheep in the big box, which looks like it going to explode as the sides are bellowing out. I tried to pull the little one out, but it was well and truly stuck in there. So I grabbed hold of the big sheep's back legs, straddled the box and started to pull. From the side it may have looked like I was up to no good. After five minutes I finally got the big one out and put both sheep in the appropriate boxes. With the tricky bit behind me, I was on my way to the Manchester airport via the M6 motorway. After ten minutes there was a dreadful smell coming from the sheep who kept farting. It continued all the way to the airport. I drove most of the way with my head out of the window.

I have many more stories about transporting animals which I will gladly share if you buy me a pint.

As of Christmas 2024, I'm still the drummer with Herman's Hermits, I'm still gigging all over the world, and most importantly - I'm still loving it. I ache a little more in the mornings, and it takes a bit longer to recover after shows, but it's been nothing short of a pleasure to be able to spend my life doing what I love to do.

The last sixty years being in Herman's Hermits has been an incredible journey and it will continue for as long as I am able.

I hope you have enjoyed reading my adventures, and I hope I see you soon at a venue near you.

Yours Jan Barry Whitwam

www.ingramcontent.com/pod-product-compliance
Ingram Content Group UK Ltd.
Pitfield, Milton Keynes, MK11 3LW, UK
UKHW011447210126
10239UKWH00020B/113